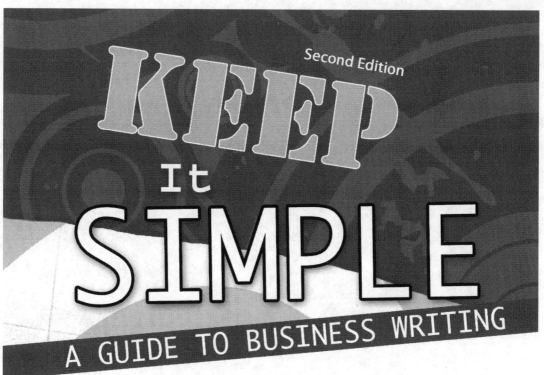

Second Edition

KEEP It SIMPLE

A GUIDE TO BUSINESS WRITING

Edward W. Hodges

University of Delaware

Kendall Hunt
publishing company

Cover image © Shutterstock, Inc.

Kendall Hunt
publishing company

www.kendallhunt.com
Send all inquiries to:
4050 Westmark Drive
Dubuque, IA 52004-1840

Copyright © 2007, 2011 by Edward W. Hodges

ISBN: 978-0-7575-9489-2

Printed in the United States of America
10 9 8 7 6 5 4 3 2 1

CONTENTS

Second Edition

KEEP It SIMPLE

A GUIDE TO BUSINESS WRITING

Edward W. **HODGES**

*For
Susan*

EXCERPTS FROM THE CHARLESTON GAZETTE

1961

A great gap in communications presents one of today's dangers to society. People don't always say what they mean. In written communications, complex sentence structure often causes misinterpretation. It can lead to embarrassing, even dangerous, results. Here are a few examples—excerpts from actual letters received by a Department of Public Assistance office (welfare) in one of our southern counties:

- "I am forwarding my marriage certificate and six children, I had a seventh, but one died which was baptized on a half sheet of paper. . . ."
- "I am writing to the Welfare Department to say that my baby was born two years ago. When do I get my money?"
- "Mrs. Jones has not had any clothes for a year and has been visited by the clergy."
- "I cannot get sick pay, I have six children, can you tell me why?"
- "I am glad to report that my husband who was reported missing is dead."
- "This is my eight child. What are we going to do about it?"
- "Please find out for certain if my husband is dead, as the man I am now living with can't eat or anything until he finds out."
- "In answer to your letter, I have given birth to a boy weighing 10 lbs. I hope this is satisfactory."
- "I am forwarding my marriage certificate and my three children, one of which is a mistake as you can see."
- "Unless I get my husband's money pretty soon, I will be forced to lead an immoral life."
- "My husband got laid off from work two weeks ago and I haven't had any relief since."
- "In accordance with your instructions, I have given birth to twins, in the enclosed envelope."
- "You have changed my little boy to a girl. Will this make any difference?"
- "I want money as quick as possible, I have been in bed with a doctor for two weeks and he hasn't done any good. If things don't improve, I will have to send for another doctor. . . ."

PREFACE

I think I've been involved with the "essence" of the principles I now teach at the college level since I was a freshman in college; many, many years ago. Our first English 101 assignment was a theme; we could choose the topic. I don't really recall my topic (probably selective memory at work), but I'm reasonably sure it was "weighty." What I do recall is getting my paper back and not finding any grade on it. Instead, the paper had red, concentric circles on it and numerous small holes. After class, I waited until the professor was free and asked what grade I had received and what the circles and holes meant. My English Prof. said that my paper was so bad that he hadn't given it a grade. Instead, he had drawn the concentric circles, pinned it to a wall and thrown darts at it! He then suggested that perhaps I should write about a topic that I knew something about. Point well taken! Some six papers later, I wrote about drag racing and, as the Prof. said, "you can practically smell the burning rubber." I got an A in the course, but more importantly, I learned some very important lessons about writing so that I could be understood.

Four years later, on my first job, I again bumped into this keep-it-simple concept. This time, my employer sent me to a company-sponsored training program on Improved Writing. The initial 2 1/2 days were spent learning how to simplify our writing through editing. The second half of the course, conducted a month later, was devoted to editing our own work in groups of four. I quickly learned the value of four editors versus one. And I got my first experience with just how powerful this concept could be.

A couple of years later, as a Personnel Development Specialist (an adult teacher/trainer), I was teaching a modified version of that course to literally hundreds of engineers and scientists. When I moved to my company's Financial Department, I found the course to be just as useful for Accountants and Financial Analysts. I have also used the principles of the course in my own writing throughout my career. When I left my employer, I began to teach my own version of this these principles to client companies and eventually, as a faculty member, to my Jr./Sr. writing classes at the University of Delaware.

And just what is this wonderful cure for what ails your writing? First of all; it's not really a writing program, it's an editing process. And, it is useful for BUSINESS WRITING ONLY! That's right, only business, not creative writing, not even casual writing, just business. Business writing is (or at least should be) writing to communicate. However, often it does not communicate, and sometimes that's because communication was not the writer's real objective. For example, the writer may have wanted to impress his/her readers with a sharp wit. Or, perhaps, the main objective was to demonstrate an extensive and esoteric vocabulary. Yet another common objective (always unstated, of course) is to provide a record. In business, we refer to this as the CYA (cover your ass) tactic. Of course, few people would admit that communicating is not their #1 objective, but that really doesn't matter. If your reader THINKS that you wrote with some objective other than communication, then you are guilty!

What this leads to is writing that is longer, more complex, and more esoteric than it needs to be; in other words, it's wordy. According to a recent survey, 90–95% of reports are from 35–100% longer than they need to be. The goal of all business writing should be conciseness. A concise report conveys all the information that the reader needs, wants, or can benefit from. It should be noted that this has nothing to do with length. A long report can be concise if it contains no extra words. Conversely, a short report can be wordy if it contains unnecessary words.

If it takes an employee longer to read and understand a fellow employee's writing than it should, then company time is being wasted. Wasted time is wasted money. Added to this is the very real possibility of serious errors, lost production, lawsuits, etc., just because someone didn't understand someone else's writing. This is usually not a problem with verbal communication because there's feedback, both verbal and nonverbal. If you say something and your listener looks puzzled or asks you to repeat or explain, you can do so immediately. If you send a letter, or e-mail, you don't have that instant feedback. In fact, you may not have any feedback, until it's too late.

Recently, some universities have begun to move toward teaching this style of writing. I can only guess that is because their clients, primarily businesses, are demanding it. And, in what I can only describe as the last bastion of the totally incomprehensible document; law firms are also starting to show interest in these principles. More about the principles as we continue.

So, that's what this book is all about. It's about writing all kinds of business documents clearly and concisely. And there's a little advice and a little bit of folklore. As I tell my students, "If you can avoid making a mistake because of something you heard here, something we talked about in class, then this course is worth my time teaching and your time learning!"

That's the objective of this book.

WRITING TIPS

"Time is money!" Is there anyone who *hasn't* heard that? Well, guess what? It's 100% completely true. If it takes other employees longer than it should to read and understand your writing, then you're wasting time. You're wasting your time writing it and they're wasting their time reading it and trying to act intelligently on it. Your writing needs to be succinct, brief, to the point, concise, (dare I say simple?). This is what "business" wants. Heck, this is what your company wants. Most of us are wordy by nature when we write. In fact, in more than 40 years of teaching writing in education and industry, I don't recall a single person who was not! The objective is not brevity; it's conciseness. In fact, a very short report could be wordy because it has extra words. And a long report could be concise because it uses no extra words. A concise report delivers its message in as few words as possible, no extra words.

And, how do you write more concisely? For starters, follow the Writing Tips throughout this book.

VERBS IN DISGUISE

You disguise a verb when you turn it into another part of speech and use a weak verb in its place. For example: "There has been a mishandling of the Rowing Club's funds." Here, a perfectly good verb, *mishandle,* was turned into another part of speech, a gerund, and a very weak verb, *has been,* was used instead. Contrast this with "Fred Johnson mishandled the Rowing Club's money." Yes, the second sentence is shorter, which helps eliminate wordiness, but look at the change in tone of the sentence. The second is more direct, to the point, and has much more impact.

EDITING EXERCISE

(Sentences Come from Cover Letters)

Edit the sentences below and make them as concise as you can. Try to get inside the head of the person(s) who wrote these and write *what they should have said.*

1. Another one of my responsibilities deals with my leadership skills in that I was in charge of creating and grading quizzes given once a week to the students.
2. In the resume that follows you will see that I am extremely qualified.
3. I can contribute to the financial management leadership at _____ and aid in the improvement of government operations.
4. I am writing you to inquire in reference to the possible for immediate or future employment with your corporation.
5. These experiences have become a great educational tool that others will able to learn by.
6. I maintain the respect and support of previous employers.
7. In addition my best grades have been in my major and minor courses, which is indicated by my _._ grade point average in them.
8. Through this personal experience, I have become familiar with the country.
9. I am seeking a challenging and responsible position within a career environment in the banking industry.
10. At your request, I will be happy to furnish letters of will inform you of my sales and management reliability.

UNNECESSARY ELABORATION

You elaborate unnecessarily when you say things that your reader already knows, or couldn't help but know from things you've said, are saying, or are about to say. "I have 25 students in class #1 and 27 in class #2; so a total of 52 people are enrolled in Creative Writing 103." Do I really need to add anything after the semicolon? Most of us can add 25 and 27 in our heads and reach the total of 52. Here's the correct sentence: "I have 25 students in class #1 and 27 in class #2."

"WIMPY" SENTENCES

Most "wimpy" sentences are caused by too much use of the passive voice. Do you remember that old rule? I'll help you: the active voice means the subject is doing the acting; in the passive voice the subject is being acted upon. "Jack threw the ball." "The ball was thrown to Jack." The issue is not using the passive voice; it's overuse of the passive. The result is writing that has no impact; it's dull, and uninteresting. In fact, if you should ever want to *"damn something with faint praise,"* or give a proposal a good chance of failing, load it up with passives!

ROUTINE DOCUMENTS

The format of these routine documents is not really that important. If your company does it a particular way, then by all means follow that format. These are usually brief letters/memos, but they can be extremely important. It might be wise to outline them even though they are short. Remember, everything you write is painting a picture of you as an employee. You want to paint an attractive picture, particularly when you're a newbie!

Always keep your addressee in mind. What does he/she need to know? Who else, if anyone, should see this? Should you CC them? What impression does this create on the part of your addressee? BCC?

Whom are you really writing for? What do you need to do to make this more useful for him/her?

REPORTS

Again, is there a certain way that reports are prepared in your company? You might ask a fellow employee or perhaps the boss's secretary/administrative assistant. In the absence of any guidance, follow the format of (1) Executive summary (so the reader can decide if this is for him/her and therefore read on, (2) Introduction, statement of the problem, (3) Body of your report, (4) Conclusion and recommendations, (5) Acknowledgments.

E-MAIL

Yes, e-mail is alive and well in the corporation, but perhaps not as the recent grad knows it. First of all, most e-mail is serious, and intended to be that way. Companies tend to have a rather limited sense of humor, and anything you send by e-mail is subject to scrutiny by just about anyone in management. As a rule of thumb, **don't put anything in an e-mail that you wouldn't want everyone to read!** That's right, there's no privacy in corporate e-mail. Think about it; you're using company computers, company time, and you're sending it to other company employees! What did you expect?

Your e-mails should be understandable and brief. If you find yourself on the second page of an e-mail consider a letter instead. Are you a devotee of all those e-mail shorthand tools, like "I'm w8in 4 U?" Forget them and, while you're at it, forget all those cute emoticons. Check your e-mails for spelling and accuracy as well as grammatical correctness. Again, as with your writing, e-mails also paint a picture of you.

ROUTINE LETTERS

Complaint Letters

Steve Jobs, President
Apple
1 Infinite Loop
Cupertino, CA

May 23, 2007

Dear Mr. Jobs,

Last May, my parents gave me an iPod Nano for graduation. It worked well for almost a year, which is what I'd expect from an Apple product. I've owned your computers for years. A couple of weeks ago, my Nano died! Nothing, no music, no video, no light, nothing. I contacted your East Coast repair facility.

Body of letter

Could you please send me a new Nano, or repair this one? *(Always make clear what you want,
what will again make you a happy
customer.)*

Yours,

John C. Jones
2843 Rutter Drive
Wilmington, DE 19898

ROUTINE LETTERS

Information Letters

John Jones, President
Jones Industries
2121 Powell Ave.
Wilmington, DE 19898

May 23, 2007

Dear John Jones, *(Never; either Mr. Jones, or John;*
not both, unless you're selling
something and want to
advertise that in the salutation)

We're pleased that you have expressed interest in our Model 101. It can handle the volume you need and yet I think you'll find it well within your budget.

(A lead, so Mr. Jones can decide
whether he should read this letter
or refer it to one of his staff.)

Body of letter

If you have any questions, please contact me at 302-279-5555.

Yours, *(Sincerely, Respectfully, Yours Truly; just about anything except, Love)*

John C. Savoni
Sales Rep.

ROUTINE LETTERS

Persuasive Letters

John Jones, President
Jones Industries
2121 Powell Ave.
Wilmington, DE 19898

May 23, 2007

Dear Mr. Jones

You need the JC Model 101. We've just increased the horsepower by 17% so that you can tackle any job in your yard or, for that matter, just about any yard.

Body of letter

This could make you the envy of the neighborhood. *(In addition to extolling your product's virtues, try to appeal to what might also be your customer's psychological needs.)*

I'll call you early next week to schedule you for a test drive.

Yours,

John C. Savoni
Sales Rep.

MEMOS

Date: May 23, 2007

To: All Male Employees *(Why send this to people
                          it doesn't apply to?)*

From: Human Resources

Subject: Paternity Leave of Absence

There will be an informational meeting on this topic on Monday, May 30 in Room 241 promptly at 2:00 PM. You can expect to be able to return to your work by 3:00 PM.
(Remember the KISS acronym? Keep it simple, Stupid!)

ZERO WORDS

TIP

4

Zero words are words that take up space in a report. They don't add anything to the meaning, in fact, some actually may mislead the reader. Finding and deleting zero words is easy. Read the sentence with the zero word; read the sentence without it. Did you lose any meaning without the word? If not, it's a zero word and you need to take it out. Here's a special tip: most of your zero words are very likely to be spelled t-h-a-t! I recommend you check every "that" you use to see if it's needed or if it's a zero word.

VERBAL COMMUNICATION

There are times when you should use verbal communication rather than writing. For example:

- For speed, nothing beats actually speaking, even in this age of lightning fast alternatives.
- When you need to get a quick response.
- When you need to get a consensus, difficult to do in writing.
- When you want to enhance a relationship, no not that kind, a business relationship. Much easier to do verbally.
- When dealing with a "sticky" personnel situation. For example, you need to correct the performance of someone who reports to you, but you don't want a record of that correction.
- When you need to persuade someone about something, anything!

So, there are numerous situations when it's better to talk. Unfortunately, communicating verbally is almost as difficult as writing. There are many things that get in the way of communicating clearly and concisely.

One of these barriers can be **body language** (BL). There are excellent books on this topic and I am by no means expert in this area. However, some of the rudimentary things seem to be known by just about everyone. Standing (or sitting) with your arms folded across your chest is an indication that you're "closed," not open to new ideas or proposals. Failing to meet one's glance is interpreted (in our society) as a sign of dishonesty. Remember that old line of dialogue in western movies: "He wouldn't look me in the eye. He's lying!"

There are also aspects of (BL) that are a lot more pleasant. A smile is interpreted in almost all cultures as welcoming, friendship, happiness. Another facet of nonverbal communication is your appearance. When you are perfectly dressed for the occasion, you tend to be more confident and self-assured. And, naturally, the converse is also true.

A caveat about body language: Be sure what you're seeing is indeed body language and not just some physical habit or tic. For several years, I worked with an executive who, in times of stress, would take off his glasses and rub his temples slowly and with a great deal of pressure. His subordinates, some of whom knew something about BL were sure that this was an indication that he was really, really upset and about "to blow." I had known Bill for a number of years and knew that he suffered from sinus trouble. That rubbing felt good! It had nothing to do with his mood or actions.

At times, movements and physical placement can be **distractions** when communicating verbally. Try to communicate with someone who's drumming on the table with his or her fingers! The way a speaker moves about on a stage can be distracting, particularly if there is a definite pattern to that movement. And the distance between you and the person you are trying to communicate with can be an issue. In our society, the "normal" distance between two people who are talking to each other is approximately 18 inches. If you vary that distance either by backing up or moving in, don't be surprised if communication suffers.

Touching is another touchy area, no pun intended! First of all: Hodges Law of Touching. Other than handshakes, in our European-American cultures, touching between the two genders is OUT! Verboten! No! Don't do it! It can be interpreted as sexual harassment and you (and your company) can be sued. It's unfortunate, because touching conveys warmth and warmth is a good thing, even in business. There are numerous studies which show that everything from babies to flowers and animals respond positively to touch. But not to man-to-woman or woman-to-man touching.

Touching within the same gender is OK, depending on the culture in your company. Do guys slap each other on the back in congratulation? Then, it's probably part of the culture and shouldn't hurt you. BUT, one very important unwritten rule: The superior can pat the subordinate on the back, but it never goes the other way. You cannot pat the boss on the back, at least not until you outrank him!

While we're on the topic of verbal communication, let's look at the **setting**s for some of these conversations and see what we can read into them. How about an impromptu meeting in the boss's office. She saw you in the hall and asked if you'd drop by her office after lunch.

Your boss's office is not as small as yours, but it's not huge either. Her desk is against one wall and two side chairs are across from her chair. She also has a small round working table with three chairs in the corner.

You enter and the boss gestures to one of the two chairs across the desk from her. You can relax; everything is business as usual. However, let's assume she suggests, "Let's go over to the table and talk." Something is up! Maybe your transfer to the worst location the company has, or maybe you've been selected to run the United Way campaign. Whatever, it's going to be different and perhaps not too pleasant.

The theory behind the above scenarios is that the boss's desk is a natural barrier between superior and subordinate, and "natural" talk occurs when you and she are in those positions. However, the round table removes this barrier and hopefully makes you more amenable to something new, very new!

There are other "location" scenarios. Suppose you need to have a very unpleasant conversation with another person on the same level as you. In fact, you plan to chew this person out in such a way that he/she will never forget it! I think most people would rather have this conversation in their office rather than their victim's. Home turf? Yes, but its more than that. You can control your turf, at least to an extent. For example, you talk to your secretary/administrative assistant and tell him/her that when your adversary arrives for "the meeting," to wait for exactly five minutes after the office door closes and then call you. On the other side of the door, your victim has just sat down and you start the conversation, or rather the lecture. You rake your opponent up one side and down the other. Just as you are winding down and the victim will get his/her chance to speak, the phone rings. You answer it, hang up and inform your adversary that you're needed immediately; the rest of the meeting will have to be postponed. You exit, leaving a very upset and frustrated victim. Do people in the 21st century actually do things like this? Believe it!

Other "settings" which can be challenging: I have attended two meetings in conference rooms that had no chairs! That's right, everyone stood around the conference table. Both meetings were brief and to the point.

Another gambit is the time of day for the meeting. I've had meetings an hour before the start of the workday. I've also had meetings that started after quitting time. All things are fair in love, war, and business!

And, assuming you have talked with the boss, you should always be prepared to take over and run the meeting. At times, the situation may call for it; your boss is suddenly taken ill and something has to be done in the meeting today. It's also possible that the boss would like to be a full participant in the meeting. It's very difficult to do that if you're also responsible for running the meeting, involving everyone, getting consensus, etc.

Finally, on the subject of settings, I attended a meeting where not one word was spoken and yet the meeting was a complete success. I am indebted to my friends at JP Morgan Chase for this experience. I attended a computer meeting with some 15–20 people. After the obligatory social period with coffee, Danish, etc., we were ushered into a room which contained small tables arranged in a circle with chairs. On the tables were computer monitors and keyboards. After we were seated, our leader from Morgan told us that a question would appear on the monitor and we were to respond to it by typing on the keyboard. We would be able to see what other people in the room were typing as well as our own contributions. As the contributions began to slow down, another topic would appear on the screen and we should follow the same process. He assured us that our responses were anonymous and asked us to respond candidly. He then left and the first question appeared before me. As I recall, the screen showed a rather innocuous question about how the recruiting process could be made more effective. Not being a very trusting type, I decided to test the anonymity feature and typed in a very terse, pointed reply about the management of the unit. No one looked at me and nothing happened, so I concluded it was indeed anonymous. My comment did seem to open a floodgate of candid responses. Visualize if you will, a room of 20 some people in a circle looking at computer monitors, and there's not a sound except the clicking of keyboards! Strange! After about 30 minutes, the questions on the computer screen stopped and a secretary entered the room. She thanked each of us for our efforts, told us we'd each receive a copy of the responses and left. A few days later, I received my copy of the responses and had to conclude that this was, particularly for Morgan, one of the most effective meetings I've ever attended. A wave of the future? I've never attended, or even heard of one of these meetings since.

There's at least one more barrier to effective verbal communication and that is the skill of **listening.** We read books and we take courses (I even teach some) in how to speak, but we rarely, if ever, consider what should be roughly 50% of communication. How can you listen effectively? How can you get past the **barriers** that both you and the speaker set up? The first step is to recognize them.

First, the setting for the communication may be a barrier in itself. Can you see and clearly hear the speaker? Are there any physical distractions in the room, sunlight in your eyes, and construction outside the open window? Are you tired? Hungry? Distracted by others in the audience? Comfortable, but not too comfortable? Recognize these and deal with them as well as you can.

Sometimes speakers create their own barriers to being understood. Beyond the banal, such as can you hear, does the speaker speak clearly, does he/she have distracting mannerisms? Are their gestures, if they have any, natural and in keeping with the topic? Are they moving about the stage, and is this movement natural? Some people have been told that it's good to move, but they move erratically, or even worse, in a predictable, hypnotic manner.

Are they using visuals? Do they need to? Are the visuals effective? Free of mistakes? Not gimmicky, i.e., PowerPoint charts where the words are flying in from four different directions with weird accompanying sounds? Can you read them? Are they "in sync" with the speaker's message?

Finally, how about the speaker's words? Are you hearing lots of "uhs," "ums," "OKs," "you knows," "Do you see what I'm sayings"? There's really very little you can do about this except to try to filter them out as you listen. By all means don't fixate on them and lose the message altogether. I once counted 89 straight times a friend ended a sentence with "you know." Amazing, right? What was amazing was that I have no idea what this meeting with my friend was about!

Perhaps the most effective barriers to be overcome are the ones we create for ourselves. We sometimes create barriers based on race or gender. Do we really listen to women who want to comment on sports topics? How about guys who have opinions on women's clothing styles? Is the young, recently hired, African American man worth listening to on the subject of inventory? How about the older, hard-to-understand, Hispanic woman who always wants to discuss company benefits? Is it just the topics they're raising that "turn us off"? Or is it the people themselves?

As mentioned earlier, the distance between speaker and listener can be a barrier. If you're standing perhaps 2–3 feet away from someone from middle Europe, perhaps an Italian, you may be insulting him or her. At the very least, they're wondering why you are so far away. Conversely, moving too close (closer than 18″?) to an Asian may be just as insulting. The problem is not the insult; the problem is that no communication is occurring!

Violating cultural norms also prohibits the free flow of ideas. I frequently tell my University seniors that if I were an Asian professor, they'd be insulting me by their posture in class. It often seems that no more than 10% of the student is actually in/on the chair!

Other's cultural norms may inhibit communication. It is not unusual for Arab men to hold hands in public. In fact, you may recall a recent visit to the United States by Crown Prince Abdullah of Saudi Arabia, President Bush actually took his hand as they walked into the Press Room of the White House. A former student (who spent four years in the Middle East) described how Arab men would also hold one of your hands as they talk to you. Honestly, how much communication do you think would go on if you were the one whose (I'm assuming for the moment that you're male) hand was being held?

Tips for listening effectively:

- Try to identify the organizational structure the speaker is using.
- See if you can paraphrase what he/she is saying.
- Try to pick up key terms and define them.
- Connect what you're hearing to other material you've heard and understand.
- Anticipate the uses you might put this information to.
- Reconfirm any controversial points with the speaker after the speech.

A sidelight to this topic is the subject of **jargon.** I would define jargon as a very effective means of communicating IF EVERYONE IN THE AUDIENCE UNDERSTANDS THE JARGON. It's sort of a shorthand method of communication. However, if you hear jargon and you don't understand, you might consider the following: Why are you hearing it? Is everyone else in the audience in the field where this jargon is used? Is the speaker using it to intimidate you? Are you loathe to ask a question? Do you think that is the intention of the speaker? Is it being done to impress you? Or is the speaker just too lazy to translate what he or she really means?

Have you ever heard a speaker use **slang or cursing** in a speech? I will do so occasionally, and always for a purpose. Sometimes it's to identify with my audience; sometimes it's to shock them. Does it work? Sometimes. However, it's extremely important to know what you can say at any given point in time. For example, five years ago, I would not dare say that what someone did really *pissed* me off. Now I can say it; it's in the language. There are certainly groups that I'd never use that word in front of, but it is now "accepted." The language changes and sometimes rather quickly. I'm reminded of the famous TV routine by George Carlin, "The Seven Words You Can't Say on TV." I think there are only two left, and no, I'm not going to name them, at least not now.

Strategies for talking:

- Use nonverbal elements appropriately.
- Be literal and direct, particularly with people from other cultures. Avoid subtleties.
- Repeat and summarize often. Unlike written communication, redundancy is OK.
- Use visuals and writing where possible.

One other strategy for talking deserves explanation. This is the time-honored principle of taking turns when talking with another person. I was taught from a very early age to talk and then shut up and listen to the other person. When they finished, then I could talk again. And how do you know when the other person is through and it's your turn? Simple, the level of their voice drops at the end of the sentence. However, in the mid 80's, a very significant event occurred in the San Fernando Valley of California. It was the advent of Valley Girl Talk. This was observed and commented upon by many people, including linguistic experts from UCB.

Valley Girl Talk is distinguished by having every sentence end on an up note. "My name is Suzy. I'm majoring in Basket Weaving. I'll be graduating in May." Note: your voice should end on a rising note at the end of each sentence. Do you see the problem this presents to non-Valley Girl Talkers? We don't know when the VG is through and it's our turn. This leads to talking over each other and lots of jumbled communication. I should note that although this started as a female phenomenon, it has now been adopted by most, if not all, of my male college students. It's used in formal presentations as well as casual conversation. We call it **Up - Talking.**

Gaining compliance (getting people to do what you say) is another specialized aspect of verbal communication. Getting people who work for you to do what you say can be surprisingly difficult. Often this style of supervision reflects our own personality and training. Many times, the style we adopt relates to our experience with our first boss. Interestingly, we seem to learn just as well from a negative as a positive example. I learned many years ago that I'm much better at persuading, cajoling, and selling people to do my bidding. I'm not effective at "chewing people out." I can do it, but it's just not my style. Others seem to adapt that style without even thinking twice. One note, my style takes time, and sometimes you don't have that luxury. If the building is on fire, I won't be persuading anyone, I'll be ordering!

There are two more aspects of verbal communication that bear mention, mainly because I don't think anyone else takes notice of them. First is the **heated discussion,** an argument, a screaming match. (Note: this screaming match cannot escalate into a physical confrontation! If it does, unless your uncle owns the company, you are an exemployee, and so is your combatant! Are we clear on that? I don't care what he/she called your mother; you do not fight!) There are things you can do to deal with a situation like this. Assume, if you will, that you're peacefully working at your desk and suddenly someone appears in your doorway and begins to rip into you, verbally in a loud voice, a very loud voice. #1. Stand up, if you remain seated, the screaming will continue. Standing seems to speed up the inevitable cessation of the diatribe. Don't move toward the person, just stand. #2. Don't scream back, talk in a normal tone. Eventually, you'll bring the screamer down to your level. #3. (Perhaps the hardest) Hear the person out completely before you defend yourself.

I'm assuming that the screamer has ceased screaming, heard your side of the story and left your office. This situation, relationship, whatever, cannot continue. This is very much against our upbringing. In grade school, you could just play on the other side of the playground and you wouldn't run into him/her. In high school, you could just eat lunch at the other side of the cafeteria and leave school by a different door. It doesn't work that way in business. That situation must be resolved; it cannot continue. The best of all possible worlds would be if you and your "enemy" could resolve it between yourselves. The next best would be if you can get a third person to mediate and it could be solved that way. The worst choice is if that the third person has to be a supervisor or manager. Now, it's on your record, even if you didn't start it.

Taking no for an answer. There are some people in this world, particularly in management/supervision in business who will say "no" to just about any suggestion or request. It's a knee-jerk reaction and it's instantaneous. (My first boss was like this.) It doesn't seem to matter what the subject is, the answer is going to be "no." Some of these individuals are aware that they have this characteristic, and no, I don't know how to spot them. If they are aware, a strange phenomenon can occur when you get that initial "no." They may think less of you for not trying your suggestion/proposal again. Subconsciously, they may think that either you didn't think it was a very good idea either or you give up too easily.

I suggest that either immediately, or a few days later (I'm assuming it was a good idea), try it again, perhaps in slightly different language. Sometimes, you'll get a "yes." However, if you get another "no," drop it. You haven't hurt yourself; in fact, you may have even gained a little.

INCOMPLETE THOUGHTS

This is saying something more than once, but less than twice. First, you say it, but incompletely. Then, you fill in the blanks from the first time you said it. Or you say it again, but this time completely. For example: "There are no naturally pink wines. Most are made by taking the juice from black grapes away from their skins while they are fermenting." What this amateur oenologist might have said was: "Most pink wines are made by separating the juice of black grapes from the skins during fermentation." Not a lot of words saved, but the meaning is clearer.

SPEECHES/ORAL PRESENTATIONS

CHAPTER 4

It's knee-knocking time! The boss just walked into your cubicle and suggested that it would be nice if you gave a short presentation during the section's regular staff meeting on Friday. She thinks this would be a good way to "introduce you" to the section. She said, "Why don't you talk on something that you're familiar with such as MySpace and Facebook? I doubt many of our people even know they exist unless they have high school or college-age kids." By the way, you don't think this really was just a suggestion, do you? No, you have no choice; you're going to be the star performer at the staff meeting whether you like it or not! You've got four days to get ready, and you've never even attended a staff meeting.

What to do, what to do? There are a number of things you can do to make this job a little easier and the finished product a lot better. In communication terms, the **context** for your talk is an *internal* one. It would be *external* if you were briefing newspeople, speaking at the annual meeting, etc. So we have an internal context for your talk.

The next thing you should do is to **analyze your audience.** The results of your analysis could make a difference in the way you prepare your speech. First, what is your audience's **purpose** for being there? If this talk were being given to a larger audience, some might be there because they're very interested in your topic, others because they have no choice. In some circles this is known as the "guided missile" approach. The boss says to employee A, "You will go to the meeting, you will listen carefully and take notes. You will then come back to our section and brief the rest of us on what happened." I'm guessing that most of the people in attendance at this meeting are there because they want to be there and it's not "good form" to miss a staff meeting.

Next, let's consider what the **mood** of your audience might be. Since we can't get into people's heads, are there any general events which might be affecting everyone's mood? For example, any "bad news" announcements lately; i.e., layoffs coming in the fourth quarter? Conversely, bonuses for everyone at year-end? These, or any one of a myriad of situations, could affect the way your audience will receive your message.

What, in your opinion, is the **attention span** of your audience? *Attention span* is a term usually used in conjunction with young children and their ability to concentrate for a specified period of time on a particular subject. Very young children may have an attention span of only a very few minutes, perhaps even seconds. That span grows as the individual gets older. Personally, I'm convinced that one's attention span is longest during college years (18–23). I can state with absolute certainty that the span grows shorter as one ages. I have taught adults in their late 50s and early 60s that had attention spans no longer than very young children. Your audience, with ages probably forming a bell-shaped curve from 18 to 60 or so, should not be a particular problem.

One more bit of analysis: What is the **rate of absorption** of your audience? This is dependent on your topic and how much you will need to do to bring the audience up-to-speed. Social networking for high school and college students on the Internet is not brain surgery; you should probably not have to slow down or do much translation for the audience.

So much for the preliminaries, now on to the talk itself. How to prepare? For you, until very recently a student in college, this may be the easiest part of the job. You certainly know how to do research on the net or in the library. I might suggest a couple of additions to your research routine. You might ask one or more of your co-workers or even better, perhaps the boss's secretary/administrative assistant some general questions about presentations in staff meetings. For example, are they very informal with perhaps a flipchart or two, or is one expected to really go all out and prepare a PowerPoint presentation? How long do you have to make your talk? The preparation for a ten-minute talk is quite different from a half-hour one. The time factor can even influence your subject. If you have ten minutes, you'll probably need all the time to describe the two sites. If you have a lot longer, you can get into the dangers inherent in these sites to students, how industry uses the sites, how the sites can guard their members' personal information, etc.

You also need to know if anyone else is going to give a talk and what the title of it is. In this manner, you can insure that your topic will fit in, or at least not appear completely inappropriate. Next, find out where the staff meeting room is and check it out at the time of day that you'll be giving your talk. Now you'll know if there are any distractions, such as sunlight coming through a window, loud persistent noise, etc., and you can deal with them.

Consider using visuals to enhance your presentation. They almost always heighten the impact of the message. But each has its own set of pluses and minuses. **Overhead transparency projectors** are easy to use and usually readily available. However, they are perhaps the least "spectacular" of visuals aids. And there is the added hazard of written errors on the transparency and/or being unable to read the handwriting of the preparer.

Back-in-the-day, speakers used **35mm slides** with their presentations. They are colorful, sexy, and easy to use. However, they have one very large drawback—you have to darken the room to use them. And, if you darken the room, you almost insure that someone will go to sleep, and may even snore!

Flipcharts which hang on hooks on the wall are effective, particularly if they're professionally made and in color. If you want to make your own as you talk, once again, you have the hazards of making a mistake on the chart or having your audience unable to read your writing.

Some speakers can work with a **blackboard** very effectively. Again, don't make any mistakes and be sure you can write legibly. Blackboards also have a built-in attention getter. If your audience is beginning to nod off, just scratch the chalk and you'll have them back almost instantly, albeit a little annoyed.

Finally, the king of them all, the Rolls Royce of presentation techniques—**PowerPoint.** Somewhere in a room, someone is making a PowerPoint presentation even as you read this. It is without question, the most powerful tool yet developed for speakers. However, it too has its problems. Paramount among those is one easily solved, locating the file with the presentation in it. If I had a nickel, a quarter, well, some amount of money for every time a presenter lost the file, I'd be able to buy Microsoft's latest version of the program. This is not a difficult problem; simply label the file clearly and leave it in one location on your machine. One further caution: PowerPoint can do some amazing tricks on the screen. Words can shoot in from the right, left, top, and bottom. Sounds can also be added to enhance these actions. I'd keep it pretty simple—no bells and whistles until you know your new company and their likes and dislikes.

OK, you've written your talk out and it's time to practice it. DON'T READ YOUR TALK! If you're reading it, you're not really giving a presentation. You could just pass out copies to the audience. Talk about your points to the audience. My favorite method is to reduce my talk to an outline and talk from that. I have a friend who memorizes talks and gives them flawlessly. Find your style of presenting and use it. Use 3 × 5 note cards for your notes; they're less distracting.

Practicing Tips

1. If possible, give your talk to a live audience—your roommate, your significant other, Mom or Dad.
2. Time yourself.
3. Get your "audience" to watch to see if you have any distracting mannerisms.
4. Practice using your equipment (PowerPoint, transparencies, etc.).
5. Get feedback and at least make an attempt to improve. It may take some time to get rid of tics, uhs, and ahs, etc.

Practice another couple of times and then give your talk. I'll bet you're going to do a great job.

By the way, did you know you could be interrupted by a question or comment while you're giving your talk? That's right; they can just throw in some comment or question while you're tossing out those pearls of wisdom. As a rule of thumb, anyone at your level in the organization (and most of the audience is) can, and may interrupt with a question. Expect it! You'll probably have to answer the question or say something like, "Charlie, I'm just getting to that topic right now." Answer the question and continue.

At the conclusion of your presentation, it's only polite to ask if there are any questions. There may be some. If so, consider them a compliment. After all, if there are questions, it means you had an interesting topic. Answer the simple ones; suggest that you'll get together later with those with detailed questions. Compliment your questioner, "Charlie, that's an excellent question." Did I mention that you can't guess at the answers or BS? No one is expected to know everything about anything. There's absolutely nothing wrong with saying, "That's a good question, I don't know. But, I'll find out and get back to you." Don't ever BS when asked a question you can't answer; it can be career limiting!

Finally, if you don't get much feedback immediately after your talk from the audience, go get some. Ask your boss a couple of days later about what he/she thought of your talk. Ask if there are any places where it could have been improved. You might also ask a co-worker, although you're less likely to get real honesty.

"INSIDER" PHRASES

These are phrases that people use for no apparent reason. Perhaps it's because they think that using them will identify them as members of a certain group. For example, they might use terms like *input* and *output,* hoping that others will think they're computer savvy! The interesting thing is that you rarely hear these words spoken; they only appear on paper. That's right, we don't talk this way, we only write these words. Some words and phrases and their more familiar translations: inasmuch as=since, therefore=so, the above-named=these people, due to the fact that=because, etc. Again, the way to spot these terms is that they only appear on paper.

WRITING/ORAL PRESENTATION ASSIGNMENT

Name _____ Date _____

Assume that your Instructor is a wealthy investor (I realize this is a real stretch, but try!). Select a stock, bond, or other type of investment for me. Research your selection and tell me (in writing) why this is the best course of action for me. You might include the history of your choice, where it is now and where you expect it to be, and when. If you feel I should invest my money elsewhere, such as charity, tell me why and why it makes business sense.

Give me a brief report (less than two pages) and be prepared to present your analysis/recommendation to the class.

ORAL PRESENTATION EVALUATION

Name _____ Date _____

Content

Presenter: _____

Intro:

Effective? Why or why not?

Discussion:

Did he/she get to the point? How quickly? Clearly?

Closing, or transition to next speaker:

Appropriate: Too brief? Too long?

Comments on Content:

Speaking Skills

Posture:

Presence? Leaning? Weaving? Ease?

Gestures:

Any? Both hands? Broad or restricted? Natural?

Voice:

Clarity? Quiver? Strong? Talking up?

Distracting Mannerisms:

"Uh", "Ah", "you know", "basically"

ATTENDING/PLANNING MEETINGS

In this electronic age, meetings are a remnant of the past, right? No, meetings are alive and well and they may even be increasing in number. As with most business topics, there is both an upside and a downside to meetings. Pluses:

- Meetings are a quick way to spread info.
- Some problems can be solved in meetings.
- Meetings give visibility to subjects without necessarily doing anything.
- They can help build teamwork.
- You can get a consensus on questions.

However, there are also minuses:

- Office politics can raise its ugly head in meetings.
- People get snubbed.
- Quiet people may not participate.
- It's easy to get off-track.
- They can be a terrible waste of time.

There are different types of meetings; most are what I'd call **regular meetings.** Staff meetings, safety meetings, corporate meetings are examples. Then, there are **special occasion meetings,** such as meetings with clients and meetings with people from other areas of your company. **Task forces** would be yet a third type of meeting. Task forces are usually made up of people (usually not more than a handful) who are to solve a problem, institute a new policy, select outside vendors, etc. In short, they have a mission and once that mission is completed, typically, they're disbanded. It's usually an honor to have been selected for a task force, but it can also be a royal PITA.

What goes on in a meeting? In addition to completing the mission of the meeting, a lot of group dynamics go on in meetings. There is usually at least a brief socialization period at the beginning where people meet those they don't know and renew acquaintances with those they do. There's usually a lot of non-business conversation ranging from gossip to sports, and you are expected to participate—at least in everything except the gossip! When the actual meeting starts, many things can occur. Leaders emerge, people adopt support roles, frequently someone will perform the role of devil's advocate, and alliances can be made and broken. If you have the luxury, it can be very instructive to just sit and watch the dynamics in a group, who does what, who usually backs whom, etc.

There can also be lots of nonverbal dynamics. Where each person sits in the room can have many ramifications. For example, the person with the most power (not necessarily the highest-ranking by title) will often sit near the middle of the table on the side; I'm assuming there is a table with chairs around it. This is so that he/she can see what every other person at the table is doing, how they're reacting to ideas, etc. Usually, the head of the table is reserved for the person leading the meeting. Frequently, to the immediate left or right of the meeting leader's chair is a chart easel. The chair next to that easel is to be avoided at all costs! Whoever sits there will probably be asked to keep notes of the meeting progress on the chart. That person will not be participating in the meeting; he/she will be too busy getting every idea on the chart, trying to remember how to spell certain words, and desperately trying to write clearly enough so that everyone can read and understand the words. By the way, the meeting leader, in a sense, is also a non-participant in the meeting. He/she has other things to worry about; such as keeping people on the subject, summarizing, getting consensus, trying to get quiet participants to actually say something, watching the time, etc. So, if you want to participate or (I can't imagine why) want to keep someone else from being an effective participant. . . .

It's time to mention an invaluable asset to the new meeting participant: Roberts Rules of Order. General Henry M. Robert, born in 1837, was a general in the U.S. Army and also an engineer. General Robert felt there was a need to bring the rules of the American Congress to everyday life so that all (most?) meetings could be conducted in the same manner. He developed his version of those rules in 1876. They were revised in 1915. Here is an excerpt from the 1915 version which is now in the public domain.

PART I.

Rules of Order.

Art. I. How Business Is Conducted in Deliberative Assemblies.

1. Introduction of Business
2. What Precedes Debate
3. Obtaining the Floor
4. Motions and Resolutions
5. Seconding Motions
6. Stating the Question
7. Debate
8. Secondary Motions
9. Putting the Question and Announcing the Vote
10. Proper Motions to Use to Accomplish Certain Objects

1. **Introduction of Business.** An assembly having been organized as described in **69, 70, 71,** business is brought before it either by the motion of a member, or by the presentation of a communication to the assembly. It is not usual to make motions to receive reports of committees or communications to the assembly. There are many other cases in the ordinary routine of business where the formality of a motion is dispensed with, but should any member object, a regular motion becomes necessary, or the chair may put the question without waiting for a motion.

2. **What Precedes Debate.** Before any subject is open to debate it is necessary, first, that a motion be made by a member who has obtained the floor; second, that it be seconded (with certain exceptions); and third, that it be stated by the chair, that is, by the presiding officer. The fact that a motion has been made and seconded does not put it before the assembly, as the chair alone can do

that. He must either rule it out of order, or state the question on it so that the assembly may know what is before it for consideration and action, that is, what is the *immediately pending question.* If several questions are pending, as a resolution and an amendment and a motion to postpone, the last one stated by the chair is the immediately pending question.

While no debate or other motion is in order after a motion is made, until it is stated or ruled out of order by the chair, yet members may suggest modifications of the motion, and the mover, without the consent of the seconder, has the right to make such modifications as he pleases, or even to withdraw his motion entirely before the chair states the question. After it is stated by the chair he can do neither without the consent of the assembly as shown in **27(c)**. A little informal consultation before the question is stated often saves much time, but the chair must see that this privilege is not abused and allowed to run into debate. When the mover modifies his motion the one who seconded it has a right to withdraw his second.

3. **Obtaining the Floor.** Before a member can make a motion, or address the assembly in debate, it is necessary that he should *obtain the floor*—that is, he must rise after the floor has been yielded, and address the presiding officer by his official title, thus, "Mr. Chairman," or "Mr. President," or "Mr. Moderator;[1] or, if a woman (married or single), "Madam Chairman," or "Madam President." If the assembly is large so that the member's name may be unknown to the chairman, the member should give his name as soon as he catches the eye of the chairman after addressing him. If the member is entitled to the floor, as shown hereafter, the chairman "recognizes" him, or assigns him the floor, by announcing his name. If the assembly is small and the members are known to each other, it is not necessary for the member to give his name after addressing the chair, as the presiding officer is termed, nor is it necessary for the chair to do more than bow in recognition of his having the floor. If a member rises before the floor has been yielded, or is standing at the time, he cannot obtain the floor provided any one else rises afterwards and addresses the chair. It is out of order to be standing when another has the floor, and the one guilty of this violation of the rules cannot claim he rose first, as he did not rise after the floor had been yielded.

Where two or more rise about the same time to claim the floor, all other things being equal, the member who rose first after the floor had been yielded, and addressed the chair is entitled to the floor. It frequently occurs, however, that where more than one person claims the floor about the same time, the interests of the assembly require the floor to be assigned to a claimant that was not the first to rise and address the chair. There are three classes of such cases that may arise: (1) When a debatable question is immediately pending; (2) when an undebatable question is immediately pending; (3) when no question is pending. In such cases the chair in assigning the floor should be guided by the following principles:

1. *When a Debatable Question Is Immediately Pending.* (a) The member upon whose motion the immediately pending debatable question was brought before the assembly is entitled to be recognized as having the floor (if he has not already spoken on that question) even though another has risen first and addressed the chair. The member thus entitled to preference in recognition in case of a committee's report is the reporting member (the one who presents or submits the report); in case of a question taken from the table, it is the one who moved to take

---

[1]"Brother Moderator," or "Brother Chairman," implies that the speaker is also a moderator or chairman, and should not be used.

the question from the table; in case of the motion to reconsider, it is the one who moved to reconsider, and who is not necessarily the one who calls up the motion. (b) No member who has already had the floor in debate on the immediately pending question is again entitled to it for debate on the same question. As the interests of the assembly are best subserved by allowing the floor to alternate between the friends and enemies of a measure, the chairman, when he knows which side of a question is taken by each claimant of the floor, and these claims are not determined by the above principles, should give the preference to the one opposed to the last speaker.

2. *When an Undebatable Question Is Immediately Pending.* When the immediately pending question is undebatable, its mover has no preference to the floor, which should be assigned in accordance with the principles laid down under (b) in paragraph below.

3. *When No Question Is Pending.* (a) When one of a series of motions has been disposed of, and there is no question actually pending, the next of the series has the right of way, and the chair should recognize the member who introduced the series to make the next motion, even though another has risen first and addressed the chair. In fact no other main motion is in order until the assembly has disposed of the series. Thus, the motion to lay on the table, properly used, is designed to lay aside a question temporarily, in order to attend to some more urgent business, and, therefore, if a question is laid on the table, the one who moved to lay it on the table, if he immediately claims the floor, is entitled to it to introduce the urgent business even though another has risen first. So, when the rules are suspended to enable a motion to be made, the mover of the motion to suspend the rules is entitled to the floor to make the motion for which the rules were suspended, even though another rose first. When a member moves to reconsider a vote for the announced purpose of amending the motion, if the vote is reconsidered he must be recognized in preference to others in order to move his amendment. (b) If, when no question is pending and no series of motions has been started that has not been disposed of, a member rises to move to reconsider a vote, or to call up the motion to reconsider that had been previously made, or to take a question from the table when it is in order, he is entitled to the floor in preference to another that may have risen slightly before him to introduce a main motion, provided that when someone rises before him, he, on rising, states the purpose for which he rises. If members, rising to make the above mentioned motions, come into competition they have the preference in the order in which these motions have just been given; first, to reconsider; and last to take from the table. When a motion to appoint a committee for a certain purpose, or to refer a subject to a committee, has been adopted, no new subject (except a privileged one) can be introduced until the assembly has decided all of the related questions as to the number of the committee, and as to how it shall be appointed, and as to any instructions to be given it. In this case the one who made the motion to appoint the committee or refer the subject to a committee has no preference in recognition. If he had wished to make the other motions he should have included them all in his first motion.

From the decision of the chair in assigning the floor any two members may appeal,[2] one making the appeal and the other seconding it. Where the chair is in doubt as to who is entitled

---

[2]In the U.S. House of Representatives there is no appeal from the decision of the chair as to who is entitled to the floor, nor should there be any appeal in large mass meetings, as the best interests of the assembly require the chair to be given more power in such large bodies.

to the floor, he may allow the assembly to decide the question by a vote, the one having the largest vote being entitled to the floor.

If a member has risen to claim the floor, or has been assigned the floor, and calls for the question to be made, or it is moved to adjourn, or to lay the question on the table, it is the duty of the chair to suppress the disorder and protect the member who is entitled to the floor. Except by general consent, a motion cannot be made by one who has not been recognized by the chair as having the floor. If it is made it should not be recognized by the chair if any one afterwards rises and claims the floor, thus showing that general consent has not been given.

4. *In Order When Another Has the Floor.* After a member has been assigned the floor he cannot be interrupted by a member or the chairman, except by (a) a motion to reconsider; (b) a point of order; (c) an objection to the consideration of the question; (d) a call for the orders of the day when they are not being conformed to; (e) a question of privilege; (f) a request or demand that the question be divided when it consists of more than one independent resolution on different subjects; or (g) a parliamentary inquiry or a request for information that requires immediate answer; and these cannot interrupt him after he has actually commenced speaking unless the urgency is so great as to justify it. The speaker (that is, the member entitled to the floor) does not lose his right to the floor by these interruptions, and the interrupting member does not obtain the floor thereby, and after they have been attended to, the chair assigns him the floor again. So when a member submitting a report from a committee or offering a resolution, hands it to the secretary to be read, he does not thereby yield his right to the floor. When the reading is finished and the chair states the question, neither the secretary nor anyone else can make a motion until the member submitting the report, or offering the resolution, has had a reasonable opportunity to claim the floor to which he is entitled, and has not availed himself of his privilege. If, when he submitted the report, he made no motion to accept or adopt the recommendations or resolutions, he should resume the floor as soon as the report is read, and make the proper motion to carry out the recommendations, after which he is entitled to the floor for debate as soon as the question is stated.

4. **Motions and Resolutions.** A motion is a proposal that the assembly take certain action, or that it express itself as holding certain views. It is made by a member's obtaining the floor as already described and saying, "I move that" (which is equivalent to saying, "I propose that"), and then stating the action he proposes to have taken. Thus a member "moves" (proposes) that a resolution be adopted, or amended, or referred to a committee, or that a vote of thanks be extended, etc.; or "That it is the sense of this meeting (or assembly) that industrial training," etc. Every resolution should be in writing, and the presiding officer has a right to require any main motion, amendment, or instructions to a committee to be in writing. When a main motion is of such importance or length as to be in writing it is usually written in the form of a *resolution,* that is, beginning with the words, "*Resolved,* That," the word "*Resolved*" being underscored (printed in italics) and followed by a comma, and the word "That" beginning with a capital "T." If the word "Resolved" were replaced by the words "I move," the resolution would become a motion. A resolution is always a main motion. In some sections of the country the word "resolve" is frequently used instead of "resolution." In assemblies with paid employees, instructions given to employees are called "orders" instead of "resolutions," and the enacting word, "Ordered" is used instead of "Resolved."

When a member wishes a resolution adopted after having obtained the floor, he says, "I move the adoption of the following resolution," or "I offer the following resolution," which he reads and hands to the chair. If it is desired to give the reasons for the resolution, they are usually stated in a *preamble*, each clause of which constitutes a paragraph beginning with "Whereas." The preamble is always amended last, as changes in the resolution may require changes in the preamble. In moving the adoption of a resolution the preamble is not usually referred to, as it is included in the resolution. But when the previous question is ordered on the resolution before the preamble has been considered for amendment, it does not apply to the preamble, which is then open to debate and amendment. The preamble should never contain a period, but each paragraph should close with a comma or semicolon, followed by "and," except the last paragraph, which should close with the word "therefore," or "therefore, be it." A resolution should avoid periods where practicable. Usually, where periods are necessary, it is better to separate it into a series of resolutions, in which case the resolutions may be numbered, if preferred, by preceding them with the figures 1, 2, etc.; or it may retain the form of a single resolution with several paragraphs, each beginning with "That," and these may be numbered, if preferred, by placing "First," "Second," etc., just before the word "That." The following form will serve as a guide when it is desired to give the reasons for a resolution:

Whereas, We consider that suitable recreation is a necessary part of a rational educational system; and

Whereas, There is no public ground in this village where our schoolchildren can play; therefore

Resolved, That it is the sense of this meeting that ample playgrounds should be immediately provided for our schoolchildren.

Resolved, That a committee of five be appointed by the chair to present these resolutions to the village authorities and to urge upon them prompt action in the matter.

As a general rule no member can make two motions at a time except by general consent. But he may combine the motion to suspend the rules with the motion for whose adoption it was made; and the motion to reconsider a resolution and its amendments; and a member may offer a resolution and at the same time move to make it a special order for a specified time.

5. **Seconding Motions.** As a general rule, with the exceptions given below, every motion should be seconded. This is to prevent time being consumed in considering a question that only one person favors, and consequently little attention is paid to it in routine motions. Where the chair is certain the motion meets with general favor, and yet members are slow about seconding it, he may proceed without waiting for a second. Yet, anyone may make a point of order that the motion has not been seconded, and then the chair is obliged to proceed formally and call for a second. The better way when a motion is not at once seconded, is for the chair to ask, "Is the motion seconded?" In a very large hall the chair should repeat the motion before calling for a second in order that all may hear. After a motion has been made no other motion is in order until the chair has stated the question on this motion, or has declared, after a reasonable opportunity has been given for a second, that the motion has not been seconded, or has ruled it out of order. Except in very small assemblies the chair cannot assume that members know what the motion is and that it has not been seconded, unless he states the facts.

A motion is seconded by a member's saying "I second the motion," or "I second it," which he does without obtaining the floor, and in small assemblies without rising. In large assemblies, and especially where non-members are scattered throughout the assembly, members should rise, and without waiting for recognition, say, "Mr. Chairman, I second the motion."

A working knowledge of these rules and others not shown above, not really all that complicated, can be invaluable in your adult life. In the absence of anything else, you'll find that most organizations operate using these rules. That can include organizations you belong to now as well as in the future, and perhaps even your company.

With this somewhat lengthy preamble, let's assume your boss has appeared in the doorway of your office and said she'd like you to set-up and run the next monthly staff meeting. You probably shouldn't feel either honored or put upon, many newbies get this job. What's your first move?

I'd have a brief talk with one of your more-experienced co-workers, or even the boss's secretary/administrative assistant. Your quest is quite simple: What are these monthly staff meetings like? What goes on? Where are they usually held? Guest speakers? A typical format? Who regularly attends? Guests? What day of the month, week? Time of day? Do they vary much? Armed with the answers, or at least a good guess, what's next?

In order, I'd select a day, and location. Now, having done so, back to the boss's right-hand-man, or -woman to see if there are any potential conflicts. Next, I'd go to that meeting location to see if there are any problems with it. Big enough for the meeting? How many seats are there and how are they arranged? If you'd like group participation, you might consider arranging them in a circle or oval. If, on the other hand you'd prefer that the "audience" simply sit and listen, try schoolroom style—rows, etc. Are there any distractions built into the room, for example, sunlight streaming through a blindless window into someone's eyes? Can you fix this, perhaps with a change in the time of day for the meeting or having blinds installed? Does the room have any necessary equipment for your meeting, for example, a PowerPoint projector?

One more logistics consideration: What time of day do you intend to hold the meeting? If early morning, I'd suggest not before 9–9:30 AM. This gives everyone time to attend to any necessities at their desks and get a cup of coffee. Recent research suggests that most people are at their best at about this time. Suppose you don't want people at their "sharpest"? Try right after lunch, 1–2:00 PM. If everyone eats lunch, particularly if the weather is cool/cold, your only distractions may be gentle snoring! Why would anyone ever want to conduct a meeting where the participants are not sharp? Suppose you have material to present that you'd prefer people simply listen to and not question. How about getting a seemingly innocuous proposal accepted?

OK, we've got the room and time of day set. Did I mention that you're going to have to send out a memo inviting everyone to the meeting? And, when you give the time of the meeting, say 9:30, you also need to state the ending time. For example, 9:30–11:00 AM. If you don't state an ending time, many people won't come; they simply can't afford the time to go to an open-ended meeting. The lone exception to this is when the ending is a natural one, for example, the meeting begins at 11:00 AM. Everyone knows the end will be at noon.

Now for that memo: you have the day, time of day, location, and people to be invited. Do you need anything else? Special guests? Perhaps an agenda? You might want to talk to anyone who's on the agenda to see what they plan to cover and how. This allows you to procure any special equipment they might need and evaluate how well this topic will fit in with others, if any, on the agenda. See the sample memo below.

MEMO

To: Procurement Section Members
From: John Jones
Subject: Regular Staff Meeting
On Friday, June 5, our regular June Staff Meeting will be held in Room 204 at 3:00 PM. The meeting will conclude no later than 4:30 PM.

Agenda: Opening remarks—Section Mgr.
Introduction of new employees—Section Mgr.
"College Socialization on the Internet"—John Jones
Announcements—Judy Johnson
Safety Tip—Sam

This should be sent to all attendees and guests at least two weeks before the meeting. The meeting went smoothly and your only worry is that it went so well that you might get this responsibility on an ongoing basis.

One more detail and you're through. Sometime within the next couple of days after the meeting, ask a couple of co-workers what they thought of the meeting. Armed with their feedback, ask your boss the same thing. Don't make a big deal of it, just a simple, "How'd you think the meeting went?" In addition to giving you valuable info in case you have to do this job again, your boss will probably be impressed by your thoroughness.

PREPOSITION LAST

If there is one grammatical rule that's chiseled in stone, it's that *you can't end a sentence with a preposition.* Of course you can, we do it all the time when we speak. If we can speak it, why can't we write it? The simple answer is that you can end a sentence with a preposition when writing if it helps you with your main job, which is to communicate. Example: ". . . the behavior in which they have been engaging."—". . . the behavior they have been engaging in." There, did the sky fall? I don't think so. The second sentence is much clearer, and it's even shorter, which helps us with wordiness.

YOU'RE THE MEETING LEADER

More about meetings! Previously, we talked about how to set up a meeting, inform invitees, etc. You spoke, but only in an informative manner, i.e., you didn't have to get agreement on something or really accomplish anything. There are other meetings with a more serious purpose. Perhaps you'll use a meeting to solve a problem.

There are probably as many ways to solve problems in a meeting as there are problems to be solved. Most experts feel that the biggest part of solving a problem lies in defining it. For example, we're getting rained on in our living room. The problem is that it's raining. Or we need an umbrella. No, these are symptoms; the problem is the hole in the roof! If you can correctly identify the problem, that often points to the solution.

The second step is to gather as much data as possible about the problem. Do our neighbors get wet standing in their living rooms? Do our friends who live in another state have the same problem? Have we always had this problem? Have we ever had this problem?

A logical next step would be to define the criteria for evaluation solutions to the problem. First and foremost, the solution must stop us from getting wet in the living room. Second, it must be a lasting solution, not just one for this storm. Third, it must have a reasonable cost. We can't move; that's too expensive. We can't erect roof above our house; that would also cost too much.

Next, we can brainstorm about possible ways to solve this problem. When we have several, we can evaluate them against the criteria we set up and see which, if any, are workable. We decide to hire a handyman to find and fix the roof leak, which is causing us to get wet. This seems to meet all our criteria.

Finally, we need to develop an implementation plan and put it into effect. We decide to call the Better Business Bureau and get recommendations on reputable handymen and call one to come out immediately.

If you are the person selected to run a problem-solving meeting, there are a few rudimentary steps to take. I suggest that you:

- Start your meeting at the appointed time
- Make a clear statement about "why we're here"
- Keep participants on target
- Periodically summarize where the group is
- Use questions to involve the quiet members of the group
- Close the meeting with a clear summary
- Close at the stated time

We live in a multicultural world. You are very likely to have co-workers who don't speak English, who live in a different time zone, perhaps on a different continent. If you find yourself conducting a meeting which involves these people, PREPARE!

Know the customs of the different participants and be sure that you are committing any faux pas in planning and conducting the meeting. Repeat frequently, redundancy is fine in verbal communication. Use visuals where possible. Be very careful with the subtleties of English. You may think that sardonic comment you made was brilliant. Your Japanese co-worker thinks you're serious!

Finally, really, when you join a company, you'll be invited to many meetings. Some are mandatory, such as orientation meetings. Others, however, you could skip without serious consequences. Don't worry, your co-workers will be only too happy to tell you that "you don't really have to go to that one." Let me suggest that you attend all meetings! That's right, all of them. And, let me further suggest that you prepare for those meetings.

You'll know the subject, it's on the invitation they sent you. Do some research on the subject. At the very least, ask co-workers what it's all about.

Now, the most radical suggestion of all: PARTICIPATE! That's right, you're prepared, get into the discussions, offer ideas; yours are probably bright and fresh. You'll stand out because everyone expects you to just sit there and listen. Surprise them, you'll be surprised what this can do for your career.

DISORGANIZATION

Wordiness is not the only sin! Disorganization is also a problem for many. The two main causes of disorganization are *failure to outline* and *failure to use a lead*. If you're going to write anything longer than a memo or a one-page letter, I strongly suggest you develop an outline. I can think of situations in business where I'd outline even a one-page letter! For example, I might outline if the letter is going to someone who is near the top of the food chain in my company. I don't think it's important how you develop that outline; I think is very important that you do so!

The **lead** is a concept right out of Journalism 101. It's usually one paragraph, although, depending on the length of the document, it could be much more. In that paragraph you give your reader all the essential elements in your story, but no detail. It is most assuredly not an introduction, which *sets the stage for what's to come*. It's at the beginning of your letter, report, memo, etc., where you tell your reader as concisely and clearly as possible all of the essential parts of your story so that they can see what's in it for them and decide whether to read on or not. Want to see a good lead? Look at the first paragraph of any story in any well-written newspaper.

CHAPTER 7

THE JOB SEARCH

A job search is one of life's most important and frustrating jobs. It's full of contradictions. The best way to conduct a job search is while you still have one. But, if you have a job, it's very difficult to find enough time to conduct a search. You really should make finding work a job in itself. Many of the most important single elements in a job search are covered in more depth in this chapter.

If you're graduating from college, the job is somewhat easier because companies are basically expecting the same thing, good basic training, someone who knows how to learn, and the vigor, energy, and strength of youth. The actual process of finding a job is actually very straightforward and direct. Assuming you have found a company that has the type of work you want, all you have to do is convince them that you are a perfect fit for the job and that you will be worth what they'll be paying you, and the job is yours.

By all means, use your college's career service center. They will have literature on all the companies that will be interviewing on campus, they can help with your resume (although you may not need that after you read the section on resumes in this book), and they may even be able to help with your interview skills. Of course, the main way they can help is in letting you interview with companies coming on campus. They are also a great source of information on starting salaries for various academic fields. Not a recent grad? Contact your campus office anyway; many offer services to alums.

Not all the good companies come to a particular college's campus. Sometimes they just don't have enough needs to justify a campus visit. Other times, for whatever reason, the relationship between the college and the company is just not good. Sometimes, the college's product is not considered good enough for the company. Sometimes, the college doesn't want its students to work for that company. The point is, don't rely completely on the college for your list of possible places of employment. Included in this section are sample cover letters for answering newspaper and magazine ads and for use when you have no idea whether the company has any openings. If you're going to do a job campaign, do a real one. Don't just mail out 1–2 resumes, mail out 20 a week.

Also in this section is material on interviewing skills, job fairs, and how to find and use personal references. Most of the material is useful for both the fresh grad and someone with experience. It could be some of the most useful reading you'll ever do.

RESUME NO-NO'S

- "My intensity and focus are at inordinately high levels, and my ability to complete projects on time is unspeakable."
- "Education: Curses in liberal arts, curses in computer science, curses in accounting."
- "Instrumental in ruining entire operation for a Midwest chain store."
- "Personal: Married, 1992 Chevrolet."
- "I am a rabid typist."
- "Proven ability to track down and correct erors."
- "Personal interests: Donating blood. 15 gallons so far."
- "References: None, I've left a path of destruction behind me."
- "Strengths: Ability to meet deadlines while maintaining composer."
- "Don't take the comments of my former employer too seriously, they were unappreciative beggars and slave drivers."
- "I procrastinate - especially when the task is unpleasant."
- "Qualifications: No education or experience."
- "Disposed of $2.5 billion in assets."
- "Accomplishments: Oversight of entire department."
- "Extensive background in accounting. I can also stand on my head!"
- Cover Letter: "Thank you for your consideration. Hope to hear from you shorty!"

PERSONAL INVENTORY

Name _____ Date _____

- Starting on this sheet, list all the jobs you've held, full and part-time (since graduating from high school). Show the company name, city where it's located, your job title (if you had one) and the time period you worked for them. It's not necessary to show the exact dates, just "summer of '08, 6/'09 – 9/'09, etc.

- Next list your job responsibilities, and note any accomplishments you had, such as convincing the Co. to stop producing an unused report.

- List the activities you've been involved in during college. Note the time periods, years are OK, i.e. 2006 – 2009. Also, make note of <u>ANY</u> positions of leadership held in the organization.

- List any honors you've received during your college career. Dean's List (semester and year), scholarships, awards, membership in honorary fraternities, and membership in academic organizations such as Golden Key, etc, are good candidates.

- List your skills. List language skills and assign a level, i.e. basic, advanced, and fluent. What other skills do you have? Computer skills? Programming? What language(s)? ERP's such as SAP? Specialized software? CPR? Certifications? Skills in operating specialized equipment?

(handwritten margin notes:)
- use career services
- use websites to look for companies
- No gaps in time on Resume
- Send Resume to the highest person who can hire you

RESUMES

The average "reviewer" spends an average of 29 seconds reading your resume and cover letter. May I assume I don't have to convince you to write clearly and concisely? This is one of the most valuable documents you'll ever develop; it's a sales tool to sell you to an employer. It won't get you a job, but it can keep you from getting one. Let's get started!

I like to use a symmetrical style for a resume, but you can also just go down the left side of the paper if you prefer. The first item on your resume is, naturally . . .

Name:

Generally, this is your first name, your middle initial, and your last name. Sometimes, it could be your first initial, your middle name, and your last name. I would suggest that you not use any nicknames or shortened names such as "Billy Bob," "Chuck" instead of Charles, "Bill" instead of William, etc.

Address:

Street #, Apt. #
City, State, Zip
Telephone #, Cell # optional
E-mail

If you're in college, you'll probably have two addresses, campus and home. Put your campus address on the left, home on the right, same lines.

Objective:

Your objective is a major heading on your resume, just like name, and should be treated the same way. It answers the question, "What kind of job do I want?" For example, "A challenging entry-level position where I can utilize my education and experience." It can be very specific ("A challenging position in Banking.") and, thanks to computers, you can specify another field when you apply to a different firm. If you're a recent grad, you simply must have an objective; some firms won't consider you without one.

Education:

Again, a major heading. The first line after (or under) Education is the name of your degree, i.e., B.S. (not Bachelor of Science) in Economics, 2008, University of Delaware, Newark, DE. Don't deviate from this form, and be very sure you have the correct name of your degree. On the next line(s) you can list your Major, Minor, Concentration, GPA (2 places, please and leave off the 4.0), Semester Abroad, and, if you have only one, Dean's List. If you have several semesters on the Dean's list, save them for a category later called Honors.

Experience:

Not professional experience, not work experience, just experience. All your experience must be shown, not just the ones you think are important. HR people like to be able to construct a timeline of your experience. If there are gaps, be prepared to explain them. The format for showing your jobs is:

Company Name	Work Location	Time Period
Johnson Inc.	Atlanta, GA	Summer '06

You show your jobs in reverse order, listing full-time, 40 hr./wk. first, i.e., Summer '06, Summer '05, December '05, Summer '05. Then, you show your part-time jobs in the same order, most recent, next most recent, etc. After showing

Company—Location—Time, you show your job title on the second line of each listing; then your job duties (or accomplishments) using only phrases, not complete sentences. For example: "balanced GL account," "supervised 3 Salary Clerks," "developed Excel spreadsheets." Use action verbs such as "balanced, supervised, developed." Follow this format until you run out of jobs. If you're in college, don't show anything from high school.

Up to this point in developing a resume, everyone should have the same categories in the same order. Now, resumes will start differing. People will have different categories, such as Honors, Skills, Activities, Certifications, etc. Now, some suggestions about how to handle these categories.

- Honors—For multiple Dean's List entries; if you only have one, show it under Education. Honorary fraternities, sororities. Scholarships won. Awards won at work.
- Skills—Language skills, usually modified by basic, intermediate, advanced, fluent. Computer skills; operating systems, programs, programming languages. Even such skills as American Sign Language, CPR, etc.
- Activities—Companies don't care how "well rounded" you are. Therefore, the only activities you can list are those which you held a leadership position in. Companies use this "leadership" experience as an indicator that you might someday be good supervisory material.

Keep your resume to one page. Use only white, gray, or cream paper. Provide no personal information, if possible. No self-evaluations, at least not on the resume. These are permitted in cover letters. Never, never put "References Available Upon Request" on either your resume or cover letters. No references to religion or politics, if possible. No references to hobbies, charities, volunteer work, unless it fits under one of the four categories. You can have absolutely no errors on your resume. Check it yourself several times and then get friends, family, significant other to do the same. It must be perfect! (See sample on page 43).

JOHN C. SAVONI

510 Ray Street	PH: (302) 995–6022	4 Niagara Lane
Newark, DE 19711	Email: REpstein@udel.edu	Oak Ridge, Tennessee

Objective   A challenging career position where I can utilize my education and experience.

Education   B.S. Business Administration—2007—University of Delaware, Newark, DE
Major: Finance   Minor: Management of Information Systems
University Honors Program   Overall GPA: 3.8 Major GPA: 4.0

Experience   2001–Present   Pennbury Power Mower   Oak Ridge, Tenn.
IT Professional
• Upgraded the computer system from DOS to Windows 98 to Windows XP
• Implemented new backup solution with disaster recovery strategy
• Documented all computer processes
• Installed IP-Based security cameras

2001–Present   R.L. Waxman, D.D.S.   Newark, DE
IT Professional
• Consulted on adding a computer system to improve scheduling, billing, etc.
• Installed three Dell workstations and a Power Edge Server
• Set up a satellite office with six computers via vpn

1990–Present   Florham Park Hardware   Knoxville, Tenn.
Salesman—IT Professional
• Created and maintain website: http://www.florhamparkhardware.com
• Installed Point-of-Sale computer system with barcode scanners
• Assisted in forecasting sales and inventory needs

Skills   • Dos—Windows 2003 Server
• Proficient in Office 2003
• QuickBooks 2005 experience
• Knowledge of programming in Visual Basic.net and Asp.net

Honors   • Dean's List (2003–2006)
• University Merit Scholar
• University Honors Program Scholar

COVER LETTERS

A cover letter is nothing more than a carrier. It's a way to get a resume into someone's hand. I've never seen one longer than one page and they usually don't survive the initial review process. There would be no need for them whatsoever, except it's not "polite" to just send someone your resume in an envelope.

On a more positive note, CL's do offer you an opportunity to mention things you left off your resume. For example, self-evaluations are a no-no on resumes, but it is not offensive to mention in your CL that you've always been a self-starter and a quick learner.

The form for a cover letter is basically the same as for an information letter. In the first paragraph, you should state why you're writing (I saw your ad in the *Morning Sun* . . .) You should also state that you're a good fit for the job. Don't forget to mention that you've enclosed your resume.

In the body of your letter, again mention that you're a good fit for the job and give a couple of reasons why. You can mention personal qualities, relevant experience that isn't on your resume, additional education, military service, and accomplishments away from college. You can also mention volunteer activities "where you didn't have a leadership role," sports, and hobbies.

Oh, if you have any "angles" use them in the CL. For example, do you have a relative who works for that company? Be sure to mention it, their name, and where they work. Do you, or does your family know any company bigwigs? Include that; i.e., "John Jones, VP of Marketing is a close family friend and suggested that I send you my resume."

Finally, in every CL you write you must include the following sentence, "I'LL CALL YOU IN A FEW DAYS TO SCHEDULE A TIME FOR US TO MEET." You can change this to make it sound more like you, but you must include it. In effect, you're telling your reader that you're going to call up and schedule your own interview. Is this aggressive? Assertive? Yes. And, it is what's expected of you. This is part of the game of getting hired.

Put yourself in the role of the person reading this. Do you want to hire someone who says, "I can be reached at ___ ___ ___. I hope to hear from you." Or do you want to hire someone who says, "I'm going to call you next week to set up my interview with you."

Personalize the CL where appropriate: "I think my semester abroad in Italy could be a very valuable experience for your office in Milan." If you have any team experience, athletic or otherwise, which doesn't show on your resume, be sure it gets in your CL. Teamwork is a real hot button in most companies.

Don't forget to again mention your interest in the job and thank the addressee for his/her time spent reviewing your resume.

George C. Lambert
3 Arrowood Drive
Wilmington, DE 19810
302-239-7459
clamb@aol.com

— Nothing from highschool on resume

June 7, 2004

Ms. Kelly Grand
Costoso, Ltd.
143 Ninth Avenue, Suite 406
Anytown, KS 67116

Dear Ms. Grand:

I am interested in the Junior Auditor position with your company advertised in the Jan. 21 edition of the *Wilmington News Journal.* I have a B.S. in Accounting from the University of Delaware and have worked in accounting with the DuPont Company for the last two summers.

I balanced accounts and handled the petty cash fund in my last assignment. I have worked with Excel for more than four years and am comfortable with all the features of the program. I'm willing to relocate as needed and love travel. I will call you in a few days to arrange an interview at a convenient time for you. Thank you for your consideration.

Sincerely,

George Lambert

George C. Lambert
3 Arrowood Drive
Wilmington, DE 19810
302-239-7459
clamb@aol.com

June 7, 2004

Ms. Kelly Grand
Costoso, Ltd.
143 Ninth Avenue, Suite 406
Anytown, KS 67116

Dear Ms. Grand:

I am interested in working as a Programmer for your organization. I am already a competent programmer even though still a student. I enclose my resume as a first step in exploring the possibilities of employment with Costoso, Ltd.

My most recent experience was designing an automated billing system for a campus magazine publisher. I designed the overall product, including the user interface. In addition, I assisted in the development of the first draft of the operator's guide.

As a Programmer with your organization, I would bring a focus on quality and ease of use to your system development. Furthermore, I work well with others, and I have some light experience in project management.

I will call you in a few days to arrange an interview at a convenient time for you. Thank you for your consideration.

Sincerely,

George Lambert

REFERENCES

For Job Searches

You need personal references when looking for a new job. For years, probably the best-known statement on resumes and cover letters was "References Available Upon Request." That is no longer true. Someone finally figured out that statement was just about as useless as it could possibly be. Two questions: "Do you have references?" "Would you be willing to give them to someone who has a good job for you?" Naturally, the answer to both questions is yes, so why waste space on the resume or cover letter saying so?

You need 3–5 personal references. A personal reference is someone who knows you well and will say nice things about you when asked. You cannot use personal friends or relatives; their opinion is somewhat suspect. You do not want to use previous employers or bosses, they will be asked their opinion of you in the normal course of hiring. For most young people, neighbors are a good choice. Also, clergy, local businesspeople, high school teachers, college professors, and your friends' parents are good choices.

Once you have selected your references, you must contact them and get them to agree to be a reference. (I have never heard of anyone declining; it's quite an honor to be asked!) Assuming they have agreed to be a reference, you need to prepare them for the job. I would suggest you send them a copy of your resume; tell them to expect it, and brief them on what kind of job you're looking for. Tell them someone will be calling them, you hope, and asking what they know about you, your character, and your suitability for employment with their company.

After you've selected 3–4 people and prepared them for the job, make your list of references. Your list (titled **References**) should include:

- Full name including titles, i.e., Mr., Ms., Prof., Rev., etc.
- Address showing house number, street, city or town, state, and zip code
- Telephone number
- E-mail address, if any
- Relationship to you, i.e., Neighbor for 15 years, Minister for 10 years, Professor in my major and Academic Advisor.

Now, fold up that list of references and put it in your pocket when you go on interviews. Do not offer it to anyone during the interview day. However, if someone asks you if you have references, give it to them and start smiling. You don't usually get asked for your references unless the company is going to make you a job offer!

INTERVIEWING

For That All-Important First Job

Carved in Stone:

- There are more people (always, regardless of the economy) than there are good jobs!
- The interview process (especially for that first, right-out-of-college job) is a game. But, it's a very, very important game and one that you simply must win!
- You'll get the job if the company thinks you'll bring more, in value, to them than the salary they'll have to pay you.

Although not all of the following are strictly interviewing "skills," they are all capable of being improved through your efforts.

Preparation

Dry Run

Appearance

Nonverbal Behavior

Answering Questions

Asking Questions

Money Talk

Mopping Up

Preparation:

This is the first step you should take after the company has scheduled you for an interview. If you don't do some preparation, you probably won't get past the campus interview. If you don't do a lot more, don't bother with the real, on-site, honest-to-gosh, full day, big deal interview!

The company (all of them that I'm familiar with) expects you to find out all you can about them, their products, their people, their policies, and their plans. Sure, they could tell you all these things during the interview day, but why waste all that time when they could be finding out all about you and deciding to make you rich with that first job offer? Why indeed?

So, how do you go about the monumental research job? Actually, it's rather easy. You're probably already thinking about the first step. Yep, you're right, go to the Internet. Hit the world wide web and start looking. If you type the company name into a good search engine, such as Google, it will probably dump you right into the web site. If, for some reason, you don't have access to a computer, Internet, etc., don't despair; there's always the public library, your school library, perhaps even your campus career services office. If you have lots of time, you could even request that the company send you literature about themselves.

What are you looking for? Information about the company, products, etc. One of my favorite sources is the old reliable Annual Report. These days, that document could be 1/2 inch thick. However, the good news is that you don't really need to commit it all to memory. You can usually find all you need in the letter in the front of the report, to the stockholders from the Chairman of the Board, CEO, whatever, telling them what kind of a year the company had, how they see themselves, and what their plans for the future are. You might also take a glance at the financial reports, just to familiarize yourself with the way they report and typical results. Obviously, those of you interviewing for financial and accounting jobs will probably want to delve a little deeper into the numbers.

Other interesting and potentially useful stuff, such as mission statements, turnover figures, AA plans, etc., can often be found on web sites. It's also interesting to review the job openings (if any) listed on the web. Are there many in the field you're entering? What levels? In other words, does this company hire a lot of people like you, and how well do they do?

OK, now, what do you do with all this newfound knowledge? Well, speaking for myself, I'm going to make notes so I don't forget the more interesting ones. Then, having done that, I am going to forget it! Don't worry, it's now in your brain, and at the very best possible time, you'll blurt out something during the interview that will signal that you have done your homework. And, that is what is important to the company, not so much what you learned, but that you made the effort. You're now well on your way to convincing them that you're the perfect candidate for that job.

Dry Run:

Interviews can present the job candidate with all sorts of logistical problems. Where is the company located? How do I get there? Traffic? Where will I park? How much time should I allow to get there? The very best solution to all these questions is to have a dry run! That is, drive to the location, find a parking place, experience the traffic, time the run, but all under noncritical conditions. I realize it's not always feasible, particularly when the company is some distance away. However, if possible, do it! You'll feel better, more confidant, assured, and that will probably lead to a more successful interview.

Appearance:

It pains me to admit that physical appearance is an extremely important part of the interview. I wish that I could say that what you know and how you express it is far more important that how you look. I'd be lying if I said so! The bad news is that neither your author nor this book can make you pretty/ handsome! But, we may just be able to keep you from looking clueless or out of place. Let's deal with the easy ones first: Good grooming—do I need to say that you should be clean, scrubbed, polished, fresh haircut, shaved, clean nails, newly polished nails (women only), etc.? If you do need to be reminded, maybe you still need a little more college time; grad school?

By the way, on the subject of facial hair, goatees, mustaches, van dykes, etc. These are now perfectly acceptable as long as they're trimmed and neat. (Not so many years ago, a lot of college hair bit the dust before interview season. We're much wiser now! <G>) I personally would not advise you to test out the Don Johnson, Miami Vice, "I haven't shaved in two days" look. Might work, might not; why chance it?

Clothing: The watchword here is conservative. We are not pushing the fashion envelope. The lone exception is if you are interviewing at a fashion house in the clothing industry. And, if you are, skip this entire section; you have a very special problem. Good luck. Why conservative? Because most of the people who will be interviewing you will be older and probably more conservatively dressed and (subconsciously, at least) want to add people to the their company like themselves. After you get the job, you're on your own; dress any way you want. If I were you, I'd pattern my dress, at least somewhat, on what other people in similar jobs wear. Or, you could network with other young, professionals about what is in vogue. Let's get down to basics:

- Women: dresses, suits, pant suits, in blue, gray, black, brown, green, and "earthtones." White, pastel shirts, blouses. Stockings, no open-toe shoes. One set of earrings (regardless of the number of holes in your ears). No perfume, cologne, or other strong scent. At some point in the day, you'll be in a small confined area with other people and even the most expensive, elegant scent can become absolutely overpowering. Not too much jewelry. If I can hear you before I see you, that's too much. Really unsure about whether a particular item of clothing is appropriate? Why not try to network and find someone who can tell you whether "6-inch spike heels are good for an interview."

- Men: suits (no sport coats) in gray, blue or black; no green or brown. Shirts in white or pastel (sorry, the Regis Philbin look is out for interviewing!), dark socks, and dark, polished shoes. Color-coordinated tie (get it when you get your Interview Suit), which is usually some combination of red and/or yellow. No earrings. Easy on the jewelry, same as the women, and again, no heavy scents such as cologne. Perhaps, a mild aftershave.

- Casual Dress: Many companies have now adopted a full-time casual dress code. This means nothing to you, the interviewee, unless they ask you to also dress "casual" for your interview. If they do; I suggest you contact one of the leading men's/women's shops in that area and ask them what "business casual" means at that company. It's almost a certainty that some of the company's employees are also customers of the shop, and you should get an excellent answer. Otherwise, dress as you would for any other interview. You may very well be the best-dressed person in company headquarters that day. That's not so bad, is it? I really only mention this so that you won't be unduly surprised when you discover that the VP of Marketing you're meeting with is wearing Dockers and a golf shirt!

The Structure of the Interview Day:

There are probably as many different types of interviews as there are companies conducting interviews. However, most on-site, home-office interviews do have some commonality. The typical structure is as follows: Human Resources: You will be welcomed by the HR person for the company, perhaps even the person who interviewed you on campus. His/her function is to welcome you to the company, relax you, and handle the details of your interview day. The HR person will check on your return trip, help you make reservations, etc. He/she will also tell you who you will be talking to and how to handle your interview expenses. (Yes, the company will pay your interview expenses.) If the HR person doesn't mention this, feel free to ask!) You will probably end your interview day by seeing this person again.

Interview #1 (Supervisory Interview): Normally, the first person you will talk to is the person who would be your immediate supervisor if you were to accept a job offer. Do I need to say this person is extremely important? If you don't impress this interviewer, the rest of the day is a waste! This is where you'll get most of the "What if" questions. You might also expect questions about your college courses, likes, dislikes, grades, etc. Sometimes, for more objectivity, the interviewer is not your prospective boss, but his/her peer, a supervisor of another area. The net result is the same. This is the most important interview of the day; if you don't wow this person, you're not getting an offer!

Interview #2 (Managerial Interview): This interviewer is often the boss of the person who conducted Interview #1. You're likely to get less questioning about your qualifications, but more about you as a person. The office will probably be a little more sumptuous and the individual a little older. You might expect questions about your family, brothers and sisters, etc. Why you chose your college, major, career objective. This person will validate the #1 interviewer's opinion about you.

Interview #3 (Peer Interview): Some twenty years ago, companies decided to incorporate an interview with someone in the organization a very short time who could empathize with the prospective new employee. This "peer" is likely to be your age or a year or two older, may be from your college, and may actually be one of your acquaintances. The theory is that you have questions that you'd like answered, but are loathe to ask a "suit" (even if he or she isn't wearing one!) For example, you may be curious about how late you're expected to work each day, but you really don't want to ask the person who might be your boss, or his/her boss. Do you have to learn to play golf? Is it necessary to socialize with fellow employees after work, etc.? You can get those answers from the "peer." One caution, no matter how much you like the peer, or how comfortable you feel with him/her, you're still being interviewed! Don't let down your guard and do or say anything inappropriate.

Lunch: First, if your "luncheon companions" don't suggest a bathroom break before lunch, mention it yourself. You need to take care of yourself. Now, on to the food.

- Alternative #1—You go to the company lunchroom with one or more employees. If your companions are sharp, one will precede you and one will follow you. Take your cues from them. If they get soup/sandwich, I suggest you do the same. However, consider what you can get which you can eat while talking. Although your companions will assure you that "We want you to enjoy your food; you're not being interviewed now!" Of course you're still being interviewed; the only difference is that you're now talking to more than one person at the same time! Pick your food accordingly. Speaking personally, I'm avoiding soup, spaghetti, etc. A sandwich, chips, perhaps lasagna? Just remember, you're going to be talking while eating it. You will not have to pay for lunch. You will also not enjoy lunch!

- Alternative #2—You're taken to a nearby restaurant by one or more employees. You arrive, are seated and the waitperson appears as if by magic with the ever-present question, "What can I get you from the bar?" When the waitperson arrives, you need to be engrossed in something else, reading the menu, checking your pockets for lint, anything except paying attention to him/her. You don't want to be the first person to answer that question. If you're not even looking up, one of your companions will answer. If he/she quickly answers, "Ice tea, please (or Perrier and lime, etc.)," you may have just been sent a signal that the employees of this company don't drink at lunchtime. Naturally, you'd order something non-alcoholic. If, however, the answer is, "I'll have a double Manhattan," you have a dilemma. First of all, if you don't drink, now is not the time to start! If you do drink and you think your "interview performance" won't be negatively affected by a drink, go ahead. You are the custodian of your body. You know what you can and can't handle. Speaking personally, I need to be at my very sharpest during an interview and I don't need alcohol. In fact, it might make me just the slightest bit dull. Again, it's your decision; make it wisely. After the drinks arrive, the waitperson again appears, this time wanting your meal order. Again, you should not be the first to order; you want to pattern your selection around what your companions are getting. You don't have to order what they do, but simply order in the same category. If they order a hamburger, you probably should not order the filet mignon. Unsure what silverware to use when in a "fancy" restaurant? Just watch your luncheon companions are using! As in the lunchroom, order something you can eat while talking almost full time.

Interview #4 (Higher Management) If you're doing well with the interviews, you may be interviewed by a higher level of management. Again, the interviewer's office is the tip-off! Large, nice furniture, big window, couch? These are the accoutrements of a higher level manager. If you're going to get a verbal offer, it might very well come from this person. The questions should be even less specific than in Interview #2.

Final Interview (HR): Wrap-up from HR. They'll tell you how (and when) you'll hear from the company. If they don't mention this, you should. They may give you information about the benefit plans, and they'll reconfirm the expense reimbursement process and give you the necessary forms. If you didn't get the business card of each person you talked with (a common practice), get the name and title of each interviewer from HR. You'll need this to write each and every one of them a brief thank-you note.

Nonverbal Behavior:

There are several different types of nonverbal behavior connected with a job interview which are seldom mentioned. One of the first things you'll do when you meet with the first interviewer is to shake hands with him/her. How is your handshake? Has anyone ever commented on it, either positively or negatively? Get one or more friends to audition you. You should be between "I can break many small bones in your hand" and the limp-fish grip. Firm, but no pain! This can be a negative for men because they are expected to know how to do this from childhood. It's rare for men to be complimented on their handshakes, but a bad one is almost always noticed. With women, a good handshake is a plus. They're not automatically expected to have a firm, definite grip. Do not gloss over this point or brush it off! Check it out!

- Posture is also important. When seated during the interview, keep both feet on the floor and don't slouch. Yes, your mother was right! You don't need to be on the edge of your seat, but you should appear alert and interested.
- Relaxing is good, but don't remove your suit coat unless you are invited to do so. Don't smoke; no exceptions! If you want to make notes during the interview, carry a leather portfolio with a note pad in it, and always ask the interviewer if he/she has any objection to you doing so.
- Eye Contact. Very important in our culture. We equate eye contact with honesty. If you don't make eye contact with someone, they are likely to assume you have something to hide or are being less than honest. It's not necessary to lock onto someone's eyes and try to stare them down. However, when asked a question, I'd suggest the following approach. As you begin your answer, look at the questioner. Then, as you continue, you might look away in a thoughtful manner. Finally, as you get to your conclusion, again make eye contact.
- Distracting Mannerisms. Many of us have annoying things we do when we talk with other people. Frequently, these are words we seemingly cannot avoid using. I have a good friend who ends every single sentence with "you know." If you're not used to this, it's very difficult to concentrate on her message because you're waiting for the inevitable "you know." "Uhs" are high on the list of annoying habits, as is "OK." And, many of us have our pet words which seem to crop up at least every other sentence. The favorite word at my university is "basically." A year or so before, it was "clearly." And we have several annoying, and grammatically incorrect idioms which seem only to be heard in the Philadelphia region. For example, people are often hailed with "Yo." Remember Sylvester Stallone in "Rocky"? People in this area also go "down the shore" during the summer months. Another one, which drives those of us over the age of 30 absolutely bonkers, is the use of "like" continuously and indiscriminately. If I hear one more time, "I was like shocked, Dude!" The word "like" should mean "similar to" or imply some degree of friendship/love/etc. Then, there's the style of communication characterized by some speech gurus as "up-talking." This is ending the sentence with your voice rising rather than falling. In our culture, the falling off in tone signals to the other person that you're through talking and it's now their turn. When your voice

rises; what is one to think? Are you through, or are you asking a question? Another label for this behavior is "Valley Girl Talk," named for the young of the San Fernando Valley who are credited with starting it.

Other annoyances include playing with the change, keys in your pocket so vigorously that it's audible. Finally, there are the various snorts, coughs, and wheezes that even your best friend won't mention unless you beg him/her to help you. These are all things that you have control of; work on them!

Answering Questions:

There are some questions that are absolutely predictable; every interviewer uses them. And, in several instances, there is a correct answer, and expected answer. Following are some typical questions interviewers ask and the "correct" answers. In the same way that you made a "dry run" to practice getting to the company's location, you might also want to practice the way you'll answer these if (actually, when) they come up. Some schools' Career Services Center, Job Center, Placement Center, etc., offer "practice interviewing" sessions. If yours does, use it. You can never get too much practice! Do not sign up for interviews with companies you're not interested in, just for the practice. It will be obvious to the company and will reflect poorly on you and your school!

Questions Employers May Ask

- Tell me about yourself! The employer's old standby; every interviewee will get this question sooner or later. The answer is who you are, what you are, and what you're looking for in a job. You give the answer without pausing and before the interviewer can ask another question. "I'm J. Fred Fargesford (if you've already met, skip this) and I'll be graduating from Podunk U. next spring with a B.S. in Accounting. I think I'd like to start my career in auditing."
- What would you like to know about our organization? Careful with this one. If you've done your preparation, you probably won't have many questions. Your answer may confirm that to the interviewer. "Gee, I visited your web site and read your Annual Report, I don't think I have any questions right now."
- Why do you want this job? There are probably requirements for this position and, hopefully, you know some if not all of them. What you want to subtly emphasize to the interviewer is that you're the perfect fit for the job. "Well, I'll have my accounting degree, I've had two excellent summer internships in DuPont's Finance department, and I love to travel."
- What do you find most attractive about this position? There are lots of good answers to this (responsibility, challenge, variety, being part of a team, etc.). What you have to avoid are the "bad" answers, i.e., vacation plan, paid holidays, easy work, etc.
- Why should we hire you? Why indeed? Because I'm a perfect fit for your job. You probably can't say it quite that blatantly, but that's the idea.
- What are your life goals? Be careful, keep your answer strictly professional. Don't succumb to the temptation to talk about family, values, retirement, etc. "Well, in 10–15 years, I think I'd like to be in management, although I've never managed anyone yet. I do know that I would expect to be doing more complex work because of my added experience, and I fully intend to continue my education." Notice that I didn't go out to the end of my career, only 10–15 years. If pushed for your ultimate goal, I'd suggest you respond by saying, CEO. Why would you want to settle for less?

- How long do you think it will take you to get your arms around this job? Another trick question. What this is really saying is, "How long will it be before you're earning the money we're going to pay you?" The "correct" answer is something like, "I'm a quick learner, always have been. I should be up to speed very quickly." If you answer otherwise, how could any recruiter, in good conscience hire you?
- Why are you leaving (did you leave) your present (last) job? There are lots of acceptable reasons for leaving a job; better money, more opportunity, more challenge, responsibility, etc. What you need to avoid are the bad answers, such as the workload, too many hours, my supervisor, etc.
- How have you helped to reduce costs? It's all about saving money in business today. If you have ever done anything to help reduce costs in any job, be prepared to talk about it. All employers, regardless of the industry, value those who can reduce their costs.
- In your current (last) job, what features do (did) you like the most? Here, again, it's the "bad" answers you need to avoid. "Good" features of a job are things like challenge, responsibility, variety, working as part of a team, etc. If you answer by listing things in the environment, such as salary, the size of my office, the vacation plan, etc., you mark yourself as shallow and not really interested in the company's goals.
- What did you think of your last boss? Watch out! They're trying to trap you. The temptation is strong to trash your previous employer; don't do it. The underlying assumption here is that if you trash him/her, someday you'll also do it to this company. Here's something you can say with an absolutely straight face and mean it. "I learned a lot from my boss!"
- What are your strong points? If you've been reading this carefully, you know the answer to this question. That's right, your strong points just happen to be the requirements of the job! Again, don't blurt it out, just reiterate your experience, degree, love of travel, etc.
- What are your weak points? The ultimate trick question. Almost everyone has heard this by now, but recruiters continue to ask it. Take a strength and turn it into a weakness. For example: "I'm a workaholic, Sir, I love to work. I live to work. If you move a cot into my cubicle, I'll live here!" You get the idea. However, so many people have heard about this tactic that some interviewers will not let you get away with the cliché answer. The response will be something like, "Oh, come on now, that's not a weakness, that's really a strength. Tell me about your real weaknesses." At this point, you need to think, quickly, about some characteristic that you are reasonably sure has absolutely nothing to do with the job you're interviewing for. "I'm really not very artistic, Sir, never have been." With apologies in advance, I'm reasonably sure that the ability to create art is not an essential quality in a beginning Auditor. Voila, you've given the interviewer his/her weakness, but not really hurt your chances for the job.

Certainly, there are thousands of other questions that may come up during the course of the interview. The ones above just seem to come up in almost all interviews. Questions must be answered honestly. However, it is not necessary to volunteer potentially negative information. You are selling yourself to a prospective employer; you are not expected to also reveal every flaw, scratch, dent, etc.

Asking Questions:

A good interview is a wonderful thing to behold and even better to participate in. It's almost like a beautifully choreographed dance with the participants moving in tandem. If you are lucky enough to have one of these, it's entirely possible that you will have no questions at its' completion. Don't ever feel as though you have to ask a question. One of the sincerest compliments you can pay the interviewer is to have no questions. Implicit in that is the fact that they did an absolutely great job of telling you everything you'd ever want to know about the job and the company.

Naturally, if you **do** have questions, by all means ask them, particularly if the answer will determine whether or not you would accept an offer. However, you might want to think about them carefully before you ask. Avoid those that relate to benefit plans and free time. Employers would like to think that such concerns are the farthest thing from your mind. Every question, and answer, paints a picture of you as a potential employee.

And, as most of us know, there are situations when you really feel you need to ask a question. For example, the interview has not gone very well, is ending early, and you feel the need to stretch it out just a bit longer. What question to ask? Below are some suggestions. Obviously, not all of these fit every situation. You may have already asked some of them. You might select a couple you particularly like and commit them to memory. Then, if you need them, you've got them. But, I repeat, don't ever feel obligated to ask questions in an interview.

Interview Questions To Ask

The Job Itself

- What are the specific responsibilities of this position?
- What is the first challenge that needs the attention of the person you hire?
- What are the resources available (i.e., budget, staff, etc.)?
- How has the job been performed in the past?
- Why is it vacant?
- What are you looking for in the person who will fill this job?
- How will the performance of the person holding this job be measured?

Key Associates

- What can you tell me about the person to whom I would report?
- What about the other people in key positions?
- How would you characterize the people who would report to me?
- Are there any plans for expansion or reduction in staff?

The Organization

- How would you describe the "culture" here?
- What is the company's growth plan?
- What does Wall Street say about this company?
- Does the company have plans for new products or acquisitions?
- Might this company be acquired?
- Is the company contemplating relocating either geographically or out of this building?

Training and Development

- Are employees encouraged to continue their education?
- Does the company sponsor personal or professional courses, seminars, and meetings?
- Is there a training period for this position?

Compensation

- When are employees reviewed?
- How are salary increases handled?
- What is your promotion policy?

Evaluating the Company's Answers to Your Questions:

Only you can really evaluate the answers you might receive to some of the above questions because you're the only one who knows what is truly important to you. Some of the ones I consider critical are:

- Why is the job vacant? Why indeed? The last two people who had it were fired? I think I'd (at least) want to know more!

- How will performance of the person holding this job be measured? If you don't find out the answer to this one during the interview, you'd better get the answer on the first day at work. This will determine whether you succeed or not, get raises, promotions, get fired, etc.

- What is the first challenge that needs the attention of the person you hire? The answer to this one will probably tell you what single quality is most important for the person who gets this job. This is another way of saying what is the most important function of the job.

- Are there any plans for expansion or reduction in staff? The answer to this can tell you a lot about the health of the company you're considering casting your lot with!

- How would you describe the "culture" here? If you haven't gotten a good "feel" for what it's like to work here during the interview day, this one may help. If you are female/minority, and you haven't seen many people who look like you during the interview day, this may be a good lead-in question before asking (in your own words, please), "How well do people like me do at this company?" Think this might "turn off" some people? If it does, and/or they don't have a good answer for you, cross them off your list. This question will not bother the employees of the company you want to make your career with!

- Might this company be acquired? If your new employer is acquired by someone else, all bets are off. Your pre-interview research is useless, and, as a general rule, you won't be as well off. No company that is the result of a merger or acquisition can possibly have as many opportunities as those which existed in the two original firms.

- Is there a training period for this job? Believe it or not, some companies hire people on a "probationary" basis. You're hired, but you're not a real employee until you've performed satisfactorily for a specified period of time, usually 3–6 months. Do I need to say that you need to know this before going to work?

- Are employees encouraged to continue their education? To most of us, this is a very revealing question. Does the company really want its people to grow professionally? Will they assist you in getting your MS/MBA? Do they allow employees to attend courses/seminars during working hours?

- When are employees reviewed? This is a subtle way of asking when new people get their first salary increase. In 99.99+% of companies, a raise invariably accompanies the first performance review; if performance isn't good, no raise. Companies are often loathe to discuss salary policy, but they will almost always be willing to discuss how they evaluate people and with what frequency.

There may be other questions on the list which are equally important to you, these are just some of the author's favorites.

Discussing Money:

During the course of the interview day, someone may want to discuss money with you. You do not want to talk about this until you have the interviewer literally drooling over the prospect of adding you to his/her firm. This usually comes up in a rather innocuous comment like, "So, Charlie, what would you expect to be paid for a job like this?" Your answer should be something like, "I'm guessing that you probably have a salary scale that would pay me very fairly based on my experience and education. I'm willing to go along with that." The interviewer would really like for you to name a figure; don't do it! There are three possible answers to that question and two of them will hurt you. If you ask for too little, you may be thought timid, or not aware of your own value. If you ask for too much, you'll be considered unrealistic and overly impressed with yourself. The only good answer is the number the company was thinking of paying you, and I'm guessing you don't have that information! By the way, that answer above is the norm in almost all the companies that you'll talk to. There **is** a salary scale and it has all the flexibility of the nose cone of a ballistic missile! So, not only is it folly to give a number, it's hopeless!

Verbal Offers:

You might receive a verbal offer during the interview day. It is done, and its intent is to blow you away and get you to accept on the spot. I would recommend you not accept immediately. Most employers will probably respect you more if you go home and think about the offer carefully and then accept it. I suggest a response such as, "Gee, I'm really flattered. I'm honored. I have really enjoyed the day and I'm very impressed with the company and all the people I've met. Naturally, I'd like to talk this over with my (parents/significant other/spouse). Can I get back to you in a couple of weeks?" If you're still interviewing, try to get as much time to consider the offer as possible. You want to talk to other companies and see what they have to offer. If you're pushed for an answer and you don't have other offers, accept the offer. Then, continue to interview up until the time you have to report to work. If something better comes up, accept it and "back out" of the first offer. Will Company #1 hate you for this tactic? Yes, for about five minutes, after which they'll never think of you again! Will you ever come in contact with them again? I sincerely doubt it.

Testing:

Several years ago, I was able to state with a fair degree of confidence that people who had worked 4 to 4+ years to get a college degree were not subject to testing. Certainly they didn't get the same kind of skill testing that a secretary or mechanic might have to contend with. Now, it's not quite so clear. Some companies actually administer intelligence tests during the interview day. I'll resist the urge to tell you what I personally think of that policy and simply say that were I CEO, the policy would be history!

There has always been "what if" testing, and that continues. By that, I mean that you are likely to be asked "Charlie/Susan, what would you do if. . . ." Most of the time, there isn't any one answer to such a question; the interviewer really just wants to find out how your mind works. The exceptions are those companies that are known for a particular philosophy or practice. For example, you'd be wise to consider employee safety first when answering such a question posed by an E.I. duPont de Nemours & Co. interviewer. "Well, Joan, the first thing I'd do in case of an explosion is to get my people out of the area in a safe manner."

I'm not aware of any serious psychological testing of new college graduates, which of course means that it probably is going on somewhere! When I say serious, I mean professionally prepared tests being administered (and evaluated) by trained professionals, preferably degreed psychologists. However, amateurs abound, and you should not be put off if that interviewer who had previously seemed perfectly normal suddenly asks: "If you were a tree in the forest, what kind of tree would you be?" Or, "If you were an animal in the jungle, what would you be?" No, I have no idea how to answer either of these, nor would I spend more than a microsecond considering how to respond. These questions, sans professional involvement, are stupid! Have fun with them. My favorite response to the animal question is to answer, "a rat," and watch the expression on the face of my pseudo-Freudian questioner. In the unlikely event that the company does want to put you through psychological testing, be happy! That costs a lot of money. You are probably going to get a very nice job offer from them.

There is one kind of testing that you definitely will undergo at some point before joining your new employer: drug testing! You will be tested; it's just a question of when. It could be during the interview day, particularly if you've come some distance to company headquarters. If you're a "local," you might be called back at some time after the interview. Or you might be tested on your first day at work. If there's a physical exam that one must pass before starting work, the drug test will probably be a part of it. And you can expect random testing during your tenure with the company.

Mopping Up:

Before you leave, find out when you can expect to hear from the company (assuming you didn't get one of those verbal offers mentioned above). Usually, HR will tell you this. If they don't, ask. Make sure you're clear on how to handle your expenses for the trip, reimbursement, etc. If you don't have the names/titles of the people you've met during the day, ask the HR person for them. When you get back to campus, you'll need them for the short, friendly, personal thank-you note that you're obligated to send to each and every one. Yes, you have to do this. It's considered extremely bad form if you don't, sort of like not thanking Aunt Jane for those Christmas socks. The bad news is that each note has to be different, and cannot be done by e-mail. The good news is that they can be very short, certainly no more than a paragraph.

One final thought: respond to rejections. You're going to get many rejection letters during this process. That's just the way the game works. If you get one from a company you really liked, consider answering it. Twice in the last year, I've seen someone get a job by doing this. What usually happens is that the selected candidate fails the drug test or his/her references are not good and the company withdraws the offer. Now they have an open job and most of the other candidates have already accepted other jobs. They may just respond to someone who acknowledged their "no offer" letter with an offer. It happens! What have you got to lose, other than a stamp and a few minutes?

WRITING ASSIGNMENT

THE INTERVIEW

Name _____ Date _____

Your assignment is to interview someone on the subject of Communication. Your subject should be (in order of preference): 1.) A businessperson, or 2.) A college administrator, or 3.) A relative.

Your general assignment is to determine how important your interviewee feels communication is, in his/her profession. Some questions you might consider asking are:

- What percentage of your time do you spend in communicating?
- Of that time, how much do you spend in each type of communication; i.e. written, oral, electronic, face-to-face, etc.?
- How important is that communication to you?
- What happens if you do it well?
- What happens if you do it poorly?
- Knowing what you now know, if you had the chance to study communication in school; what would you concentrate on?
- In terms of communication, what would you like to be able to do better?

Your paper should be written as a narrative, that is, in story-form. <u>Do not</u> simply state your question and your interviewee's response. Your paper should be long enough to cover the subject.

Name _____ Date _____

MOCK INTERVIEW ASSIGNMENT

Please answer the following questions about your "dream" job as completely and accurately as possible. This is the job you want immediately after college; not the "CEO of large multinational conglomerate" you hope to reach in 20 years. Your answers to these questions will form the basis for a mock job interview. (If you're going to grad school; describe a summer internship you want.)

1. What is the title of your desired position?

2. What organizations have these jobs? Is there one of these that you'd particularly like to work for?

3. Where is this organization located?

4. Why THIS particular organization?

5. Do you need a college degree for this position? What kind?

6. Do you need experience for this job? How much? What kind?

7. What is the main function(s) of this job?

8. What are some other responsibilities?

9. When did you decide that you wanted to do this? Why?

10. What is most appealing to you about this job? (Pay, work, advancement, etc.)

11. Is there anything else I should know about this job to conduct an effective interview with you?

JOB FAIRS

"We see real value to them! We're only known for recruiting one type of candidate, when in reality, we need many different kinds of people. It gives us a chance to press the flesh and encourage certain candidates to come and sign up for our on-campus interviews."—Recruiting Manager for a large, multinational corporation.

Job fairs have been around for years and are either a godsend or a curse to both employer and potential employee, depending on which category you fit in. Employers construct a desk/booth with appropriate corporate logos. The affair is usually held in a large, open hall under the auspices of the school's placement service over a 1–2 day period, and all interested students are invited to attend. They meet company representatives, present their resumes, and get the answers to rudimentary questions.

From the company's point of view, these "dog and pony shows" are expensive, necessary, and sometimes valuable. Usually, but not always, held on-campus, it can cost an employer $2,000–$4,000 to participate in a 1–2 day fair. The company must ship its Job Fair booth to the campus, operate it for the duration of the fair at a cost of approximately $1,000/day per recruiter, and also pay the school a fee of perhaps $250–500 for the privilege. These costs can escalate dramatically when the fair is sponsored by a national professional organization rather than an educational institution, particularly if said organization is composed of minorities. The fee alone can be as much as the total cost of a campus fair.

Other common recruiting "tools" are presentations to campus organizations, pizza parties for campus professional organizations and societies, and even tailgate parties at football games. Most employers still feel that the job fair is perhaps the most productive of these since most, if not all, of the attendees are interested in a job with at least one of the participating companies.

And how do students view job fairs? As you might expect, there is a wide range of opinions. On the plus side:

- "They can be helpful; they get your name out there."
- "The mini-interviews were good; I'd never been interviewed before."
- "I heard that some people were hired on the spot."
- "It's pretty cool; seeing all your 'drunken' friends all dressed up and wearing business suits."
- "It's good practice, the closest thing to a real interview."
- "You can make some good connections; I was interviewed later by some of the same people that I met at the fair."
- "Job fairs give you a contact person for that company and can also lead to an immediate or 'on-campus' interview."
- "They give you a chance to get to know companies you may have otherwise overlooked."
- "Even recruiters who were looking for people with different backgrounds than mine were happy to talk with me."

However, not everyone loved them:

- "They're all the same and they're not fun."
- "You have to fake it, be over-friendly, it's like Rushing."
- "You want to stand out, but you don't know how."
- "Many recruiters—

- didn't even know what jobs were open in their own company."
- didn't seem to know about majors and schools at our university."
- seemed to be interested only in engineers."
- just gave out brochures and told us to log onto the web for information about their company."
- seemed overwhelmed; didn't seem interested in anyone."

- "It's hard to appear natural."
- "It's hard to work up the nerve to approach those booths."
- "No one actually ever called me after I gave them my resume."

And just how does this litany of good and evil relate to the teacher of Business English? As teachers, adults, and jobholders, we owe it to those who will follow to help them make sense of such rites of passage as the campus job fair. In my Jr./Sr. level composition class, we do more than just make sense of it; we teach skills that can help the student win at this bizarre, yet critical part of the game called getting a job! Some of the areas we cover are:

Resume/Cover Letter—A resume won't get you a job; but it can rule you out of one! There are hundreds of books on this topic and even templates in most word processing programs. I won't attempt to teach the subject here; but I will highlight some "immutable" principles.

- Since the average resume/cover letter receives a full 29 seconds attention from the reviewer(s), it simply must be written clearly and concisely.
- Don't say anything on your resume or in your cover letter about "References."
- Your resume should fit on one page.
- It must be absolutely correct in both spelling and grammar: no errors!

The Handshake—There is no excuse for a poor handshake. This is something that anyone can get feedback on from his/her friends. Then, it's a simple matter to learn the correct technique and practice. Note: this is equally important for men and women. Again, more later.

Eye Contact—Another biggie! In our culture, you simply must make good eye contact with the Interviewer. Although we'd never admit it, we secretly don't trust people who don't make good eye contact.

Posture—"Sit up straight, Johnny!" Does that have a familiar ring to it? Well, your mother was right. Again, people make assumptions based on what they see. If you're slouching, you can't be really interested in the job. Or maybe you're just lazy.

The Two-Minute Drill—This one, just like the NFL's hurry-up offense, is useful in several situations; it's dynamite in job fairs! It's comprised of the answers to three separate questions, which you deliver (without stopping), and in no more than two minutes. The questions are:

- Who are you?
- What are you?
- What are you looking for?

A typical Two-Minute Drill might go as follows: "I'm John Jones. I will graduate from the University of Delaware next May with a degree in Business Administration. I have had two summer internships in accounting, and I think I'd like to work in Auditing."

Job fairs can be your friends if you're prepared and follow a few simple guidelines. These were supplied by one of my graduating seniors:

- Be aware of what companies will be there.
- Focus on visiting your "favorites" first.
- Dress "up" with a suit, and look presentable.
- Bring plenty of copies of your resume.
- Polish up your Two-Minute Drill.
- Have a goal in mind, i.e., a second interview, an invite to company headquarters, etc.
- Enjoy yourself!

THE JAWBREAKER

Did your HS writing teachers tell you to come up with new and innovative word choices as often as possible? Were you chastised for using the same word twice in a paragraph? Were essays essentially a vocabulary contest? If the answer to the preceding questions is yes, then you're going to love this! **In a business document** you should never use a particular word if there is a more common, shorter, simpler, less complex word that means *exactly* the same thing. If the proposed substitution does not mean exactly the same thing as the original, then you don't have a jawbreaker. If it does, then it's a jawbreaker and you need to replace it with the shorter, simpler, word. Some examples: purchased – bought, acquired – got, raced – ran, convention – meeting, etc. How often do you make these changes? Every single time you encounter a jawbreaker, you have to eliminate it, even if it happens twice in the same sentence.

INFORMATION SHEET FOR NETWORKING QUESTIONS

Name _____ Date _____

1. How did you break into the field?
2. Where do you see a person like me fitting in the (field, company, industry)?
3. How should I prepare for a job interview in this field?
4. Who are the recognized leaders in this field?
5. What professional societies or associations should I join?
6. What's a typical career path for someone coming in at my level?
7. What are the largest obstacles I would face in this job?
8. What professional publications on this field should I read?
9. Which other professionals should I contact?
10. What kind of compensation could I expect in the first year?
11. What are the necessary skills for this job?
12. Is there formal or on-the-job training?
13. How can I best utilize the education I have?
14. How is hiring in this field done? Through the grapevine? Through direct application?
15. Can I keep in touch with you?

REMEMBER, YOU'RE LEARNING ABOUT YOUR FIELD, JOB, INDUSTRY, ETC. THIS IS **NOT** A JOB INTERVIEW!

PERFORMANCE REVIEWS

A number of years ago, I engaged a rather well-known behavioral scientist to meet with the management of my department at DuPont. Dr. Scott Myers of Texas Instruments an excellent speaker with many unique views of corporate America. In a Q & A session, one of our accounting managers asked Dr. Myers about how to give constructive criticism. I will never forget his response; it went something like this: "If your employee is really sharp, he/she will thank you for your constructive comments and may even say that his/her only regret is that you didn't speak up sooner so the employee could have already been working on correcting the flaw. Meanwhile, mentally, he/she has added your name to the top of a list which is entitled *People to Be Killed.*"

There is no such thing as "constructive" criticism; there's just criticism and none of us like it! This is why there are so many different ways of preparing for and conducting the annual (usually) performance review. The reader should, at this time, multitask and visualize the following as both a giver and a receiver.

Immutable Principles

- Both the supervisor and employee should have a clear understanding about what the job entails and how performance will be measured.
- There should be no surprises in a performance review. That is, the supervisor and employee should discuss changes in behavior when they are observed, not wait until the annual review.
- There should be work goals and objectives that the employee and his/her supervisor have set jointly. These should be challenging, but attainable.
- Do I need to say these should be in writing and both supervisor and employee should have copies? They should also be "modifiable" if both parties agree.
- There should also be personal development goals for the employee such as training, attending seminars, etc., and the supervisor should be committed to making these happen.

Guidelines

- The employee shall not be required to do a self-evaluation. If, as an employee, you are required to do so, do not under any circumstances reveal something which can be used against you. Come up with a "deficiency" which has little if anything to do with your job.
- Reviews should be conducted during working hours in a private setting with only one member of management in attendance.
- The manager/supervisor should take notes during the review and give the employee a copy.

- The employee should be allowed to read the written review and express agreement, disagreement, and additions to the write-up.
- The employee should not be required to sign the write-up indicating agreement with it.

Tips for the Supervisor

- Keep the focus on the behavior, not the individual. "It bothers me when you arrive at work late because I have to get someone to do your job." Not, "Why are you always late?"
- Always ask why a particular behavior is occurring; sometimes there's an excellent reason.
- Ask how you can help the employee accomplish his/her work better.
- Let the employee know that you're invested in him/her succeeding, that you look good when they do.

Tips for the Employee

- Approach the review with a positive attitude. After all, this is intended to help you become better, which should lead to raises/promotions.
- Don't reveal personal information that has nothing to do with the job.
- Assume, until told otherwise, that you've had a great year and that you're the best employee in the organization.
- Ask how you can help your boss realize his/her goals through your work.
- Ask if there are things you could do to enhance your value to the company.

OVER/UNDERSTATING

Part of communicating clearly and effectively with your co-workers means correctly identifying the level of seriousness of your subject. If this were done consistently, a host of problems might be averted. Perhaps it can best be illustrated by the following: "There's a funnel cloud in the distance, perhaps we should continue our baseball game at a later time," "I don't have money enough for a beer; I'll bet the GDP is in trouble, too." In each case the level of concern is obviously far from correct!

ODDS AND ENDS

Some of the items covered here are of monumental importance to the modern corporation. Their position in this book is an indication of just how important I think they are to the new, young employee. Yes, you need to be aware of them, you need to know how to handle some of them, but many are just common sense.

Diversity—According to Wikipedia, diversity in a corporate sense is when the company attempts to get the demographic of its employees to match the market they serve. (This is one reason why I think Wikipedia is almost entirely useless as a source of information.) My employer, DuPont, for many years produced mostly raw chemicals and fibers, which were then used by other companies to produce consumer products. What kind of "diversity demographic" should they have? Their customers were other companies! Most progressive companies that I'm familiar with have a different view of diversity. It's a given that there is a great deal of talent in minority groups. Minorities don't usually look to major companies when seeking employment. History would show that they had little success when they did. This means that those companies are not getting some good talent, and forward-looking managers would want to correct that. Assuming you're going to sell more products to a particular group because you have employees who are members of that group is silly.

From your standpoint as a relatively new employee, do an internal check and be sure you don't have any overt prejudices. Work on getting rid of the hidden ones you may have, but by all means, treat all your fellow employees in a fair and supportive manner. To quote a very wise vice president, "That's just good manners!" To do otherwise is career limiting! If you are able to confront your assumptions about people who are not like you and resolve them, you'll open up an entirely new world of relationships and learning. You may occasionally hear that some employee got a particular job because he or she is a (name your own minority group). I can guarantee that's not true; no company is going to endanger the bottom line just to showcase a particular minority employee. So, if that minority employee is just as talented as a "majority" employee, why did he/she get the job? Did someone discriminate in favor of them? Possibly. What's wrong with that? We've discriminated in favor of white men for 200 years! Relax! If you're as good as you think you are, no one else is going to beat you out based on the color of their skin, ethnicity, religion, gender, sexual orientation (Have I left any out?), etc. If you get the opportunity to "mentor" a minority, either formally or informally, do so; it will help your career and you may find you really enjoy it.

Managing Time—Let's cover the easy stuff first. The stated working hours for your job are 8–5 with a 1-hour lunch period. Now, what are the real numbers? When you report to work, you might ask a co-worker when he/she comes to work and leaves at night. Perhaps, you'll hear 8–5, but probably not. Usually only support people arrive and leave at the stated times. (This is because if they came early and/or worked late, they'd have to be paid overtime.) Why would you want to arrive early? Well, perhaps to get ready to start work. Perhaps to get a cup of coffee and read the Sports section of the daily newspaper before starting. Perhaps to make some phone calls and clean up some detail work from yesterday. And, perhaps because *your boss comes in at this time or slightly later.*

And why would you stay late? Perhaps to finish up a particularly difficult or time-critical job. Perhaps because this is the only time you can talk with a co-worker or consultant who can help you with a certain work problem. And perhaps because *your boss usually doesn't leave before this time.* As a general rule of thumb, it's not a good thing for the boss to come by your office and find that either you have not arrived yet, or have already left for the day. This can get ridiculous. (I once had a boss who held staff meetings at 7 A.M.) But, the advice still holds!

Lunch hours are equally hazardous. I would advise you to stay strictly within the one-hour limit, unless you're having lunch with your boss or some other member of management. Sometimes lunch at your desk can be a really nice break. You don't have to go anywhere; it's quiet, inexpensive, and you can read the paper, check out your portfolio on the web, in general, just chill! And, while we're discussing lunch, be very careful about consuming alcohol at lunch. In some companies, this is definitely a no-no. Even if it's not prohibited, consider the effect it might have on your performance in the afternoon. Once again, what do your co-workers do?

How about when you don't have enough time to do your job, or you have too much. This can be a touchy subject. Ideally, you'll get assignments, help in learning how to do them and plenty of time to really do them well. However, that's one situation out of a possible three!

Let's assume you don't have enough time to finish assignments at work. This may be normal for this company, department, etc. Ask a co-worker you trust whether you're supposed to take work home. Don't assume here; there may be security concerns with taking work off-site. You might also ask your co-worker how long it took him/her to do a similar assignment. If you do determine that you have too much work or can't meet deadlines, you need to do something! Talk to your supervisor; he/she may have inadvertently given you too much or even failed to notice how much you have "on your plate." Don't wait too long to do this. When you've just missed a deadline is too long. Much better to explain why you might be late than to explain after you are actually late. Ask your boss about what your priorities should be. What has to get done by when, what can slide a day or two, and what can be put off until you have spare time. Also you might consider describing how you're doing a particular assignment and asking if there's an easier way. You may find that the Accounting Section, not you, usually does a complex spreadsheet. Needless to say, you do not want to waste a minute while you're at work. Get a good book on time management and see if you can adopt some timesaving habits, such as handling a piece of paper that comes to your desk only once.

Too much time is an entirely different problem. I'd suggest you ask a friendly co-worker if this is "normal." Assuming your friend says it's not normal, I'd consider asking the boss if there's something he/she needs done. Perhaps a study that needs to be done, but isn't critical enough to warrant a regular assignment to someone. Be careful how you handle this; it could be interpreted as criticism of your boss's supervisory skills. You might say something like, "I've finished the report, and it was really interesting. Is there anything else that I might help out with?"

Let's assume, for the sake of argument, that your co-worker told you that what you regard as a slow pace is normal and most people enjoy it. If you go to the boss and ask for more to do, you will be "showing up" your co-workers. After all, if a newbie can produce at a higher level, so can everyone else. Now, presumably, all your co-workers will not be happy with you and you can expect a very lonely existence. The solution: I'm not sure there is one. You could use the extra time to add more detail to your analyses, reports, etc. Longer term, you might try getting an internal transfer to another work area.

If you consistently finish before everyone else and the boss is aware of it, you'll be guilty of what is called in the factory, "breaking the rate." Factory workers are sometimes paid by the number of units they produce in a given period of time. If they produce more, they get paid a bonus. If the workers can fool the industrial engineer who is setting the rate at which they get paid, the potential is there for lots of bonus money. Everyone will be exceeding the rate. But, if one worker is much faster than the others, the engineer will set the rate higher, thereby reducing the bonus. This can be a complex and confusing question for the new employee.

Personal Appearance/Dress—We established some rather extensive rules about how to dress for the job interview. I suggest you follow those same rules your first day or two at the new job. You should dress conservatively and do not push the envelope. Pay very close attention to how your boss dresses. (This is difficult/useless? if you and your boss are different genders). If there's a wide age gap between you, this may also pose some difficulties. But, if he/she dresses in a certain style, you could do worse than emulate him/her. By all means, don't deviate so much from the boss in dress that people will think you can't possibly be from the same company. By the way, it may be useful to pay some attention to people in the organization who dress/appear radically different from everyone else. They will generally fall into one of two categories. Either they are absolute "star players," so valuable to the organization that they can wear anything. Or they're losers, and you'll be able to spot them just as easily. The accountant who keeps his hair length over his collars and has a favorite fire engine red sport coat. . . .

Personal appearance is also an important consideration. Earrings? I'd follow the same procedure recommended in the interviewing section. I'd keep tattoos covered, if possible. Your hairstyle should also be no more radical than the one you had when you were interviewed. Naturally, you'll want to be well groomed at all times. As you become more comfortable with your new company and job, you may decide to change either your appearance or mode of dress. But you'll do that after careful observation and thought. Don't let something as simple as your clothing get in the way of your success.

Company Culture"What's it like to work for this company?" The answer to that question will usually reveal just about everything you need to know about the company's culture. Is it laid-back, formal, frenetic, militaristic, anarchical, hard working, smart working, etc? Hopefully, you got the answer to that question before you accepted the job offer. If not, you need to find out, and quickly. It's not really important what the culture is like, it's just important to see if you can fit into that culture and flourish. If not, work hard, keep your head down, and start looking for a new job.

Being a "Good Employee"—In general, you owe your employer a good day's work for a good day's pay, and nothing more. You should put forth your very best effort for the company and safeguard its secrets. You should follow your supervisor's direction unless it is illegal or immoral. Don't ever think that you can hide behind the "I was just following the boss's orders" defense. If it's wrong, don't do it, no matter who told you to. You should be loyal to your firm and always behave in such a manner as to benefit it.

However, you do not owe your employer your loyalty at the cost of your own well-being. If you get the opportunity to move to a better position with a better company at a better salary, DO IT. It would not only be unwise, it would be stupid to fail to take advantage of an opportunity on the assumption that your present employer will give you the same thing at some point in time. Your employer is just as likely to eliminate your job as give you a raise. When you've given your best effort and gotten paid, you and the company are even. The days of joining a company after college and retiring with the same company ended in the later part of the last century. The current projections are that most people will have as many as four different careers that might encompass working for many companies.

Teamwork/Leadership—At this point in time, teamwork is very important to many different companies in differing industries. Being able to be a good team player can mean the difference between success and mediocrity. If you have ever been on any kind of a team, be it the chess team or varsity football, you know what it is to be a team member. Suffice it to say, you must be willing and able to sacrifice your own gain for the good of the team. When you're new, you'll be expected to be an effective team member. Later, perhaps, you'll get the opportunity to lead a team. It is just as important to be a good follower as it is a leader. Most of us get the chance to be both at some point in our careers. Try to learn from watching others as they function in both roles, both those who succeed as well as those who fail. You can learn from either.

AND A REPRIEVE

Are you wondering how to start to write something with all these rules, suggestions, etc. to follow? The good news is that you don't have to. In fact, if you do, you probably won't get anything written. Paralysis by analysis! Actually, this whole process is a method of editing, not writing. So, get it down on paper and don't worry about it. It doesn't matter what you write, you're going to come back and edit it, using these principles, perhaps several times. In time, with practice, you'll be able to write, edit and re-write faster than you now write. And, as an added bonus, you'll communicate clearly and concisely. One caution: Using this style of writing/editing makes it obvious whether you really have anything to say!

THE CHURCH BULLETIN

The following items appeared in the weekly bulletin of one of our local churches. No, thankfully, they didn't all appear in the same issue.

- Don't let worry kill you—let the church help!
- Remember in prayer the many who are sick of our church and community.
- For those of you who have children and don't know it, we have a nursery downstairs.
- This being Easter Sunday, we will ask Mrs. Martin to come forward and lay an egg on the altar.
- Next Sunday, a special collection will be taken to defray the cost of the new carpet. All those wishing to do something on the new carpet may come forward and do so.
- A Bean Supper will be held next Sunday evening in the fellowship hall. Special music will follow.
- At the evening service tonight, the topic will be "What is Hell?" Come early and listen to our choir practice.
- The flower on the altar this morning is to announce the birth of David Alan Hunter, the sin of Rev. and Mrs. Hunter.
- The United Methodist Women have cast off clothing of every kind. They may be seen in the church basement this Friday from 9 A.M. to 4 P.M.
- The Low Self-Esteem Support Group will meet Thursday at 7 to 8:30 P.M. Please use the back door.
- Ushers will eat latecomers.
- Today's Sermon: HOW MUCH CAN A MAN DRINK? with hymns from a full choir.
- Potluck supper: prayer and medication to follow.
- Weight Watchers will meet at 7 P.M. Please use large double door at the side entrance.
- Pastor is on vacation. Massages can be given to the church secretary.

ADDITIONAL ASSIGNMENTS

WRITING ASSIGNMENT

Name _____ Date _____

Assume that you are to attend a regular meeting of your favorite club. You intend to try to convince them to hold a charity ball. This club operates using Roberts Rules of Order. Describe, in detail, what will happen as you attempt to get the club to go along with your idea. What will you say first? What will the Chairman say? Then, what will happen? And, after that?

What will happen if your idea falls flat? What are the points in the process where it could fail and what would be the dialogue associated with that?

EMAIL ASSIGNMENT

Name _____ Date _____

From the following list of topics, select one, which you deem suitable for the medium and send your Boss (me) an email. Make up your own position on the topic, issue, etc. (if needed) and be sure to use effective business writing principles.

1. A request to me to purchase new chairs for the reception area of your office.
2. Your proposed vacation dates for my approval.
3. Your observations on the company's affirmative action policy and procedures, for review by the top managers.
4. A change in the reimbursement policy for employees using their own cars on business trips.
5. A proposed restructuring of the firm to be considered by the board of directors.
6. Price updates for the toy section of a department store.
7. Company policy on unsolicited gifts from vendors.

INTERIM PROGRESS REPORT TO MANAGEMENT

Name _____ Date _____

Your Project Group has now been working on your major research project for several weeks. Management, your bosses, want to know how the project is coming along. You need to make a brief verbal report to them (the rest of the class) about:

- Briefly describe your project for them. What are you trying to do?
- Describe the process you're using to solve the problem.
- Where are you in that process?
- Any problems? Successes? Surprises?

INSTRUCTION SHEET FOR GROUP WORK

Name _____ Date _____

You should have a copy of each paper for each person in the editing group plus one for me!

1. Select one of the papers to work on.
2. Everyone, including the author, should read the paper.
3. The author should explain the context for the paper, what he/she was trying to accomplish, any special circumstances, etc. The other two "editors" should ask any pertinent questions.
4. Start the editing process, by going over the subject paper looking for instances of the things which make writing Wordy, i.e. Mutilated Verbs, Saying What Goes Without Saying, etc.
5. Examine the paper for evidence of Disorganization. Find the outline structure. If there was none, organize the paper. Write a lead for it.
6. Go over the paper for examples of Hypercomplexity, i.e. Sesquipedaliums, Run-on Sentences and Failure to use the Proper Level of Abstraction. Correct them.
7. The author is the final authority on all changes to his/her work. He/She must agree before anything can be changed. Authors are encouraged to be flexible with the only people in the world who could find fault with such an incredible document!
8. The author is responsible for getting the revised paper re-typed and giving everyone, including me, a copy of the vastly improved edition!